Composition Practice: *Book 4*

A Text for English Language Learners

LINDA LONON BLANTON

University of New Orleans

Heinle & Heinle Publishers
A Division of Wadsworth, Inc.
Boston, MA 02116 U.S.A.

The publication of *Composition Practice, Book 4* was directed by the members of the Heinle & Heinle ESL Publishing Team:

Erik Gundersen, Editorial Director
Susan Mraz, Marketing Manager
Kristin Thalheimer, Production Editor

Also participating in the publication of this program were:

Publisher: Stanley J. Galek
Editorial Production Manager: Elizabeth Holthaus
Associate Editor: Lynne Telson Barsky
Project Manager: Sloane Publications
Manufacturing Coordinator: Mary Beth Lynch
Photo Coordinator: Martha Leibs-Heckly
Interior Designer: Carol Rose
Cover Designer: Cyndy Patrick
Illustrators: James Edward
           Jeffrey Brown
           Ruth Osborne

Blanton, Linda Lonon, 1942–
Composition Practice, Book 4/Linda Lonon Blanton.
p. cm.
Rev. ed. of: Intermediate composition practice, Book 2. 1981–1983
ISBN 0-8384-4075-4
1. English language—Textbooks for foreign speakers. 2. English language—Composition and exercises.
I. Blanton, Linda Lonon.
1942–   Intermediate composition practice. II. Title.
PE1128.B5893 1993
808'.042--dc20   92-41832
                                                        CIP

Heinle & Heinle Publishers is a Division of Wadsworth, Inc.

Manufactured in the United States of America
10 9 8 7 6 5 4 3 2 1

Contents

U n i t 1

Describing Physical *Details*   2

Composition Focus: Physical description

Organizational Focus: Spatial order

Grammatical Focus: Present tense/Prepositions

Preface

Composition Practice: Book 4 is the fourth of a four-part writing program for adult learners of English as a second language. It is written for high-intermediate students who plan to use English for academic and/or professional purposes. The lesson format of *Composition Practice: Book 4* has been successfully tested on high-intermediate adult students of various linguistic backgrounds in intensive ESL programs.

The series begins with *Composition Practice: Book 1*, designed for use with beginning or near-beginning ESL students. *Composition Practice: Book 2* and *Composition Practice: Book 3* carry students from narrative writing on topics related to daily life into expository writing, where personal experience is viewed with an analytic eye and plumbed as support for abstract concepts and assertions. *Composition Practice: Book 4* continues the focus on expository writing and on the academic/literate behaviors required for students' academic success.

In each book of the series, the lessons are sequenced and graded, with lexical, grammatical, and rhetorical elements continuously recycled and reinforced. The series is likewise spiral, with each book beginning at a level of complexity and proficiency slightly below that at the end of the preceding book. The exercises in each lesson work the same way: The beginning exercises double back to a less complex, more narrowed focus than those at the end of the preceding lesson. This internal and external arrangement allows for review and assimilation time; it ensures that students will have no gaps in their learning; and, finally, it gives students moments to recoup psychologically, before they again push to do what they could not do previously.

The series is designed to be used in the order of its titles, although any book can be used alone. The level designations "beginning," "high beginning," "low intermediate," and "high intermediate" are intended as guides, not definitions. In reviewing the series, teachers should match the proficiency level of the materials with the intended proficiency level of a class, regardless of labels. ESL programs tend to differ considerably in their use of such terms.

Composition Practice: Book 4 is divided into ten units, each built around a reading. The reading serves to immerse students in a brief but complete treatment of a topic that will likely engage their interest. It also exposes them to new language, provides content for language work, and, above all, provides a context for talking and writing.

To the Teacher

The Series

Teachers are urged to read the prefatory remarks in *Composition Practice: Book 3* to understand the linguistic and pedagogical foundations of *Composition Practice: Book 4*. *Composition Practice: Book 4* is the last book of a four-part series designed to take ESL students from beginning to a high-intermediate level of composition work. *Composition Practice: Book 3* commences at the crucial turning point in students' development as writers, where they must make the transition from narrative writing on topics related to daily life to expository writing, where personal experience is viewed with an analytic eye and plumbed as support for abstract concepts and assertions. *Composition Practice: Book 4* guides students through this transition. At the end of *Composition Practice: Book 4*, students should be ready for the final push toward native-writer competency.

Composition Practice: Book 4

Composition Practice: Book 4 continues the emphasis on expository writing begun in *Composition Practice: Book 3*. Five of the ten units in *Composition Practice: Book 4* concentrate on the most versatile expository strategies used by writers of English to analyze, explain, define, contrast, compare, and observe. In the remaining units, writers narrate, argue, and describe.

Rather than labels for frames into which writers mold their ideas, the terms "narration," "description," "argumentation," and "exposition" connote *intentionality* on a writer's part. For example, a writer sets out to relate or narrate a set of events, thereby calling into play elements of the language that lend themselves to narration.

The readings in *Composition Practice: Book 4* can all be analyzed for discourse features that signal their writer's intentions. Students are guided through each text in the Notes and Questions section of each unit in order to raise their awareness of the resources available to them as writers of English. More importantly, however, the readings in *Composition Practice: Book 4* immerse students in a brief but complete treatment of a topic that will likely engage their interest. The readings are not presented as models for student writers to imitate; textual analysis should not reduce the readings to formulae by which the writing process can be automated.

Above all, the readings in *Composition Practice: Book 4* provide a context for talking and writing. Students must be encouraged to look within their own experience and knowledge for connections to each reading. Articulating these connections, both orally and in writing, is more important than the rhetorical, grammatical, or lexical particulars of a printed text. Teachers are encouraged to explore students' reactions to the texts as readers, rather than attempt to "teach" the texts.

Inherent in English discourse, regardless of a teacher's pedagogical stance, is the hierarchical tension between *generality* and *specificity*. This hierarchy can be seen in larger segments of essay writing, where an introduction classically narrows to a controlling idea; it also operates in smaller pieces of text, where a writer may develop a point by supporting with examples. Throughout *Composition Practice: Book 4*, exercises designed to help ESL writers develop hierarchical flexibility follow the readings: Students are required to coordinate and subordinate, generalize and support, broaden a concept and then narrow it, and reduce information and combine it.

An Overview of Discourse and Composition Practice: Book 4

The units of Composition Practice: Book 4 can be aligned with a four-part classification of discourse as follows:

1. Exposition	Unit 3:	Analyzing Patterns
	Unit 4:	Making Meaning Clear
	Unit 6:	Seeing Differences and Similarities
	Unit 8:	Observing Cause and Effect
	Unit 9:	Defining Concepts
2. Argumentation	Unit 10:	Arguing a Point
3. Description	Unit 1:	Describing Physical Details
	Unit 7:	Describing a Process
4. Narration	Unit 2:	Framing Events in Time
	Unit 5:	Posing Hypothetical Situations

In actuality, no text is exclusively exposition or description, no piece of writing is exclusively narrative or argumentative. Writers setting out to narrate events, for instance, likely describe and explain along the way; they might even do a bit of persuading. For teaching purposes, however, we may classify texts in one category or another. While this is an artificial division, it is pedagogically viable when texts are viewed according to their writers' perceived intentions, inferred from analyses of the texts themselves.

Teachers need to keep in mind, however, that rhetorical terms become important to students only as they aid in their understanding of concepts, and as they signal to writers the kind of rhetorical treatment expected of them. For example, when a student majoring in education is asked on an examination to discuss *the effects of dyslexia on a child's learning to read*, the phrasing of the task itself triggers a certain rhetorical response.

Composition Practice: Book 4 in the Classroom

Each unit of *Composition Practice: Book 4* is designed to provide material for four to five hours of class work, with some of the reading and exercises completed as homework. ESL or EFL students who meet every day for composition class can then finish one unit per week. This schedule includes reserving one of the class hours for writing, as the final most important activity of a unit. Students who have time to write more than one essay a week can be assigned additional writing tasks out of class.

Enough exercises are included in each unit to provide an "accordion" effect for lesson planning: All exercises can be assigned for the full expansion of a unit, or the work load can be reduced if some exercises seem unnecessary for a particular group of students or if time is short. The same effect is built into the instructions and suggested topics for writing essays: Students may write one essay in each unit, or more can be assigned.

Instructions and explanations in the units are directed to students; and every effort has been made to keep them simple and brief. The intent here is to avoid the often distracting paraphernalia that takes students' time and attention away from actual activities; Emerging writers can more effectively discover for themselves how English works in the actual "doing" than from reading what someone tells them about the language. Teachers should feel free to supplement, however, in cases where particular students need more assistance than is provided in the book.

Implicit in the arrangement of each unit is the importance placed on extended writing. Students analyze a reading and examine certain of its features in order to apply a growing awareness of English discourse to their own writing. Through the exercises following the readings, students focus briefly on specific features in order to manipulate them in their own writing.

Even while still attempting to grasp the myriad of discrete elements of English, students must continue to wrestle with whole compositions on a regularly scheduled basis. In writing, the whole surely exceeds the sum of its parts: An increasing proficiency in writing emerges developmentally— sometimes in small increments, sometimes in bursts—and it can only happen when writers engage themselves in the meaningful use of whole language. Students' time spent on writing-related tasks cannot substitute for time spent on actual writing.

Teachers need to build as much collaboration as possible into the writing process. Students should be encouraged to work together as writing partners— brainstorming with each other before beginning to draft; later, reading each other's drafts and responding as readers; and, still later, interacting as editors and even proofreaders. Class writing can best be carried on in a workshop atmosphere.

A Suggested Time Frame for the Lessons

If students meet five days a week, a class might proceed through each unit as follows:

Pre-first class

Students are guided through the visuals at the beginning of each unit, briefly discussing the anticipated topic and establishing a context for the reading that follows. For homework, students read the text and complete the exercise that follows.

First class

In pairs, students collaborate on the exercise assigned as homework; if they disagree on an answer, they go into the text to resolve the disagreement. Next, the teacher guides students through the Notes and Questions section, keeping the interaction free-flowing and lively. Students should be encouraged to ask other questions and comment on other aspects of the text that come to their attention. The teacher asks students to connect the content and/or context of the text to their own experience and knowledge; students articulate these connections. As time runs out, selected exercises are assigned as homework.

Second class

The exercises assigned as homework are checked, with students collaborating in pairs or with designated students working at the board. If a common problem emerges, the teacher conducts a mini-lesson to solve it. If time permits, an additional exercise or two is completed in class; the remaining exercises are assigned as homework.

Third class

As in the second class, the exercises assigned as homework are checked. Again, the teacher seizes the opportunity to conduct a very brief mini-lesson if a common confusion emerges. As little time as possible is devoted to the exercises in the third class, leaving ample time for students to make entries in their journals or writing notebooks from the list following Exercise E. An additional entry or two is assigned as homework.

Fourth class

In small groups, students share some of their journal entries and respond verbally, as readers, to each other's writing. They might point out similarities or differences in the content of their entries, recall a similar experience, and so on. Ample time should be reserved to prepare for the next day's writing workshop: Students preview their writing instructions, check over possible topics, do some thinking, confer with their partners, do some more thinking, and so on— brainstorming, making notes, and making choices as the writing process gets underway. If research on a topic needs to be done, it is done as homework. A teacher may also want students to write a rough draft at home to help clarify their own thinking on a topic.

Fifth class

In a workshop atmosphere, students write, both conferring with partners and working individually. The teacher circulates, serving as a resource for writers at work. Before the end of the class period, students need to have wrestled their writing into a draft that can stand as "final," until/unless there is more time to work on it. After last minute changes, drafts are exchanged, so that each student reads at least one other student's completed draft. Before leaving class, students are directed to turn in their drafts or add them to their portfolios.

If students meet fewer than five hours a week for writing, more of the middle matter in each unit can be assigned as homework, or left out altogether. Alternatively, more than a week can be spent on completing a unit of the book. In any case, teachers must preserve class time for students to interact as readers and writers. Students' responding to a text and a workshop-oriented writing session lie at the heart of each unit/lesson.

In *Composition Practice: Book 4*, essay exam instructions are included after every third or fourth unit. Depending on the type of instructional program, teachers might want to give periodic practice exams to acclimate students to writing without a unit's worth of immediate preparation. Teachers should feel free to use these exams or not, or to change the frequency as best suits their own program needs.

Evaluating Student Writing

Teachers are encouraged to read and respond to student writing rather than to correct and grade it. Feedback to student writing is best provided in the form of written response to the content or, better yet, in individual conferences. If grades are necessary, they should be given on compositions designated for that purpose, such as the practice exams or drafts especially selected by students from their portfolios. If students select from their portfolios, they should be given an opportunity to work further on their drafts before turning them in for grades. Grading and correcting students' writing can kill students' desire to experiment and take risks, effectively destroying the developmental nature of progress in writing; for that reason, teachers should grade as rarely as possible and only then by prior arrangement with students.

We teachers, as writers, know that most writing is never really finished; we either run out of time, lose interest, or reach a plateau where a particular text is the best we can make it for the time being. With that in mind, student writers should be encouraged to return to their portfolios periodically to pull out a draft that they feel inspired to work on further. Every piece of writing is then viewed as a work-in-progress; and a teacher's system of evaluation should not discourage this kind of initiative.

TO THE STUDENT

Welcome to *Composition Practice: Book 4*

You are probably in a hurry now to go on to a higher level of English. Undoubtedly, you are ready to achieve the academic and professional goals you have set for yourself in English.

Language Skills

In your future academic and professional writing, you will be expected to know how to do the following:

1. You will be asked to describe physical details and to describe how something works:

    EXAMPLE: *Where does a suspension bridge get its support? How does a water tap regulate a flow of water?*

2. You will be asked to relate events:

    EXAMPLE: *What led to the beginning of World War I?*

3. You will be asked to analyze—factors, types, uses, ways, causes, and effects:

    EXAMPLE: *What are the different types of cancer treatment?*

4. You will be asked to define:

    EXAMPLE: *What is dyslexia?*

5. You will be asked to hypothesize:

    EXAMPLE: *What would happen if the world supply of oil and gas were reduced by 50%?*

6. You will be asked to compare and contrast:

    EXAMPLE: *What are the differences between diesel and gasoline engines?*

7. You will be asked to reason through a certain position:

    EXAMPLE: *Are nuclear power plants safe? Why or why not?*

The Plan of *Composition Practice: Book 4*

With your future academic and professional writing needs in mind, this textbook is organized as follows:

1.	How to describe physical detail	Unit 1
	How to describe a process	Unit 7
2.	How to relate events	Unit 2
3.	How to analyze	Units 3, 8
4.	How to define	Units 4, 9
5.	How to hypothesize	Unit 5
6.	How to compare and contrast	Unit 6
7.	How to reason through a position	Unit 10

In each unit, you will read. Then you will analyze what you have read. Next, you will do exercises that prepare you for your own writing. Then, you will receive instructions for your composition and suggestions for a topic. Finally, and most importantly, you will write.

Your Compositions

Before you write, be sure that you understand your topic completely. Don't be afraid to ask if you do not understand an assigned topic. If you are unsure of your topic, your writing will be unclear. Think through the points that you want to make in your composition; some will become clearer to you as you write.

Be sure to read your compositions carefully after you finish writing. Always try to save a few minutes for this. Make changes and corrections as time permits. Become your own editor and proofreader! This is important.

Be sure that your composition *looks* good. It should look like the work of a serious student. The margins should be neat and clean. Your paper should be of standard size, 8½ x 11 inches. Try to make your handwriting clear. If you take pride in your work, your reader will consider your ideas more seriously. Good luck!

Acknowledgments

I want to dedicate *Composition Practice: Book 4* to ESL/EFL colleagues around the world; to my ESL colleagues at the University of New Orleans, who typify the dedication and commitment of professionals in our field; and to Mackie and Jordan Blanton, who have remained supportive and cooperative through the years it has taken to write and rewrite the series.

Composition Practice: *Book 4*

Unit 1

Describing Physical
Details

The Cooper House ▶
(back view)

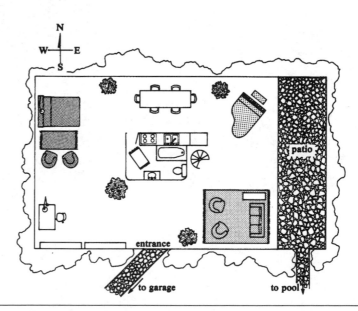

The Cooper House ▶
Homewood, Illinois

Composition Focus: *Physical description*

Organizational Focus: *Spatial order*

Grammatical Focus: *Present tense*
Prepositions

Study the photo and diagram below. What do they show? Based on the photo, what do you think you will read about? Identify the areas and items in the diagram.

● Does anything seem unusual?
● What is the title of the reading on the next page?
● What does the title tell you about this diagram?

A Glass House

(1) The Cooper house, near Homewood, Illinois, is an example of modern architectural design. The design is innovative, yet it is extremely simple. The house is basically a glass box. Because the four walls are glass, there seems to be no separation between the interior of the house and the surrounding woods.

(2) The interior of the house covers 1,800 square feet, or 167 square meters. The interior space is completely open, except for an enclosed area in the center. Here, a wall encloses a bathroom. A portion of the wall wraps around the back of a counter which serves for cooking and food preparation. The space flows in a circular pattern around this central area.

(3) In the southwest corner of the house, to the left of the main entrance, is a study area. In this area, there are several low bookcases and a desk. Over the desk hangs a chrome lamp. Next to the study area is a sleeping area. Here, two beige linen swivel chairs face a large bed. Attached to the bed is a headboard with shelves. An enormous chrome lamp arches over the bed. Between the chairs and the bed lies an orange and brown handwoven rug. The swivel chairs can also be turned to face the study area.

(4) Nothing separates the sleeping area from the eating area except a small potted tree. Here, as throughout the house, plants bring the outside in. From the dining table, positioned in front of the cooking counter, diners can see through three sides of the house. Adjacent to the dining area stands a baby grand piano. From here, music can float throughout the house.

(5) The living area, in the the southeast corner, is as simply furnished as the rest of the house. It contains only four pieces of furniture positioned on a beige wool rug. Between the living area and the rounded bathroom wall is a circular staircase. The staircase descends to two additional bedrooms and a bathroom below ground.

(6) The clean interior of the house complements the simple exterior. The two work in harmony to create a sense of pleasant openness. This openness allows the Cooper family to be part of the wooded land on which the house rests. In the winter, the Coopers can sit at their dining table and watch the snow fall. In the spring, they can watch the dogwood trees bud and flower.

Author's note: The glass house is real. It is located near Homewood, Illinois, about 15 miles (24 km) south of Chicago. It is still occupied by the architect who designed it and had it built about thirty years ago. He and his wife have raised four children there.

Please complete the outline below with information from Reading 1.

The Glass House: an example of modern design

    I.   The design of the house

        A. innovative but simple

        B. basically a glass box

            1.

            2.

    II. Open interior

        A. size: 1,800 square feet / 167 square meters

        B. layout of the house

            1. enclosed area in center

                a._____

                b. counter for cooking and food preparation

            2. area around center

                a._____

                b. sleeping area

                c._____

                d. living area

Let your teacher guide you through the following notes and questions.

1. A writer has to establish the direction of movement in a spatial description:

   - front → to back or back ← to front
   - top ↓ to bottom or bottom ↑ to top
   - left → to right or right ← to left
   - left side ⌢ around to right or right side ⌢ around to left

   Some movement is straight (horizontal or vertical); some is circular.

   On the diagram below, use arrows to mark the writer's movement through the glass house in Reading 1:

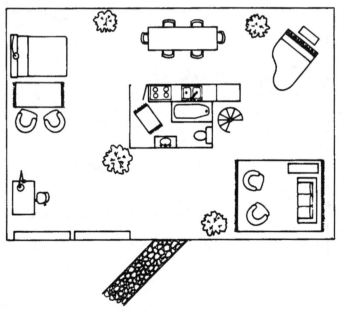

   How would you characterize the movement? Is it horizontal, vertical, or circular?

2. A consistent direction of movement is important. Also important is the tight sequencing of your sentences. This means that you usually introduce something new in relationship to what you have already introduced:

   EXAMPLE: *To the left of the entrance is* a study area. ⇄ *In this area,* there are several low bookcases and a desk. ⇄ *Over the desk* hangs a chrome lamp.

3. The spatial sequence must be tight, but this doesn't mean that the sentences that establish the sequence have to be physically end to end. A tight spatial sequence without details is dry and boring:

Boring!

   EXAMPLE: *To the left of the entrance is a dresser. Next to the dresser is a closet. Beside the closet, there is a nightstand. In front of the nightstand and beside the bed is a rug.*

Details help to create an atmosphere and show how the writer feels about the space:

More interesting!

   EXAMPLE: *To the left of the entrance is an old oak dresser that once belonged to my grandmother. It is one of my most cherished possessions. Next to the dresser is a closet, which I try to keep orderly. I can't say that I am always successful, however. Next to the closet is a pretty yellow nightstand. This is where I keep my alarm clock and a few books for bedtime reading. In front of the nightstand and beside the bed lies a beige wool rug.*

4. In Reading 1, you will find a lot of spatial vocabulary. Check the following list to make sure that you know these useful words and phrases:

above	from	on
across		on either side (of)
adjacent to	here	on top (of)
against		outside
along	in	over
around	in back (of)	
at	in front (of)	surrounded by
attached to	in the center (of)	surrounding
	inside	
behind		to the left (of)
below	near	to the right (of)
beneath	next to	there
beside		through
between		under

You and your teacher might want to play "I Spy" with these words. For example, "I spy something yellow (perhaps a pencil?) on the floor next to Maria's desk." If you don't know this game, ask your teacher for instructions; she or he will probably know it.

Now, go on to the exercises. They will help prepare you for your own writing.

Exercise A: Using Prepositions in Statements of Location

Study each picture below to figure out the position of a certain object. The first word or group of words to the right of each picture will identify the object you are trying to situate. The second word will identify the place. Use *there is/are* to state the location of each object.

EXAMPLE:

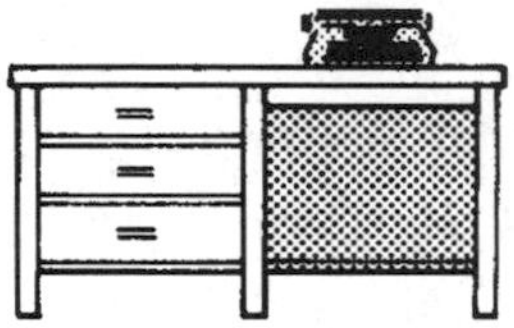

typewriter/desk
There is a typewriter on the desk.

1. night tables/bed

2. rug/table

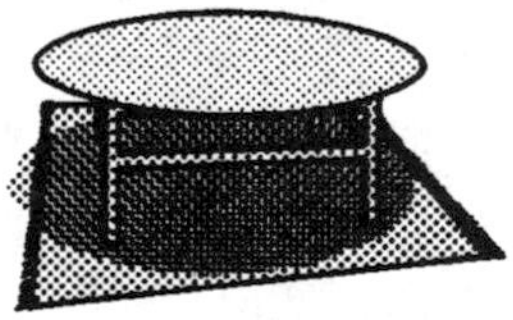

3. picture of my parents/sofa

4. long table/sofa

5.

books/bookcase
books/shelves

_____

_____

_____

_____

6.

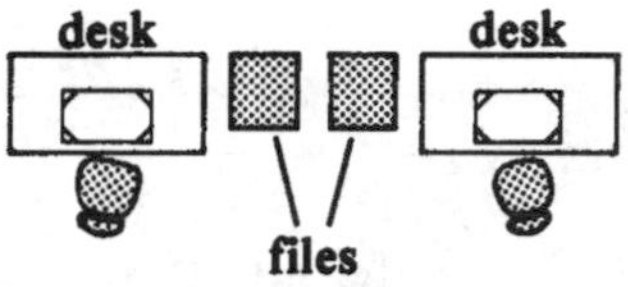

desk   desk

files

filing cabinets/desks

_____

_____

7.

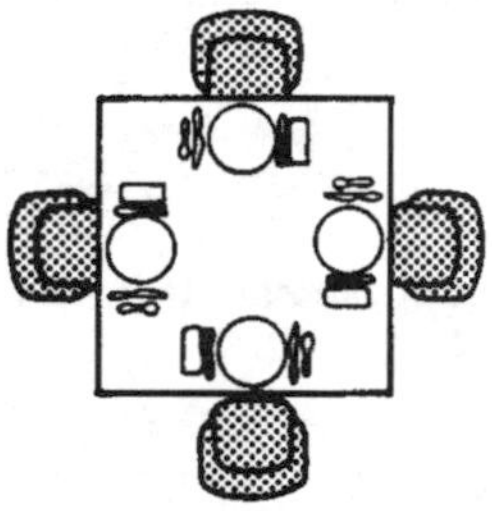

chairs/table

_____

_____

8.

dishes/cabinet
dishes/shelves
coffee cups/wine glasses

_____

_____

_____

_____

Exercise B: Stating Location

Rewrite the following pairs of sentences as single sentences. Change the verb in parentheses by adding -ING to it. The pattern that you will practice looks like this:

$$\boxed{\textit{There is/are}} + \boxed{\text{noun/noun phrase}} + \boxed{\textit{-ING}} + \boxed{\text{prepositional phrase}}$$

EXAMPLE: *There is a clock. It is on the wall. (hang)*

There is a clock hanging on the wall.

1. There are stacks of books. They are on the floor. (lie)

2. There is a ladder. It is against the side of the house. (lean)

3. There is a light. It is over the dining room table. (hang)

4. There is a large wooden bookcase. It is against the north wall. (stand)

5. There is a brown-striped sofa. It is in front of the fireplace. (sit)

6. There is a large chrome lamp. It is over the bed. (arch)

7. There are soft pillows. They are on the sofa. (rest)

Exercise C: Using Passives to State Location

Verbs such as *locate*, *situate*, *center*, and *place* are often used in the passive voice to state location. When you use them to give present location, follow this passive pattern:

| aux. *be* (pres.) | + | past participle |

Study the diagrams below to figure out how the items are positioned. Then, answer the question that goes with each diagram. Change the verb in parentheses to the simple present passive construction.

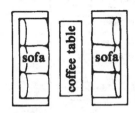

EXAMPLE: Where is the coffee table? (*place*)

It is placed between the sofas..

1.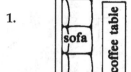

    Where is the coffee table? (locate)

    _____

2.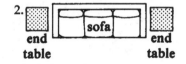

    Where are the end tables? (place)

    _____

3.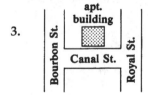

    Where is the apartment building? (locate)

    _____

4.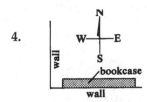

    Where is the bookcase? (situate)

    _____

5.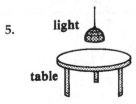

    Where is the light? (center)

    _____

Exercise D: Ordering Spatial Information

Study the drawing of the south wall of Susan Clymer's living room. Then read the list of sentences following the drawing. The sentences describe what you see in the drawing, but they are out of order. Reorganize the sentences and write the correct order, using a separate piece of paper. (**Note:** There is more than one way to organize the sentences.)

1. On the second shelf there are picture albums.

2. Susan found the shells on a trip that she took to the Caribbean last winter.

3. On either side of the bookcase stand stereo speakers.

4. On the bottom shelf are cassettes that Susan has collected over the years.

5. On the top shelf of the bookcase are dictionaries and encyclopedias that Susan uses in her schoolwork.

6. The albums contain photographs of Susan's family and friends.

7. On the south wall of Susan's living room stands a large, oak bookcase.

8. The vase was a birthday gift from Susan's mother.

9. On the third shelf, there is stereo equipment—a tape deck and a receiver.

10. Between the dictionaries and encyclopedias is a picture of Susan's niece who lives in California.

11. Whenever Susan wants to relax, she puts one of her favorite cassettes on the tape deck and lies on the floor in front of the speakers.

12. Next to the cassettes is a wicker basket full of seashells.

13. There are also art books and a crystal vase on that shelf.

14. This equipment is Susan's most valued possession because she dearly loves music.

Exercise E: Writing Spatial Descriptions

Read the following paragraph about a person named Donna Rogers:

Donna Rogers is a legal secretary who works for the law firm of Hillman, Dressell, and Axelby. She is a pleasant, hardworking, efficient employee. Her bosses depend on her to keep the office running smoothly. The top of Donna Rogers's desk shows how busy she is. It is always full, but she keeps it neat and orderly. Her desk says a lot about her and her work.

You can tell that the paragraph is an introductory one: It begins with a general presentation of Donna Rogers and narrows down to one point in particular—the top of her desk as an expression of the person and her duties.

Choose seven items on Donna Rogers's desk and use them as the means of continuing the essay about her. Remember that the top of Ms. Rogers's desk says something about her and her work: she is a *legal secretary*; she is *pleasant, hardworking,* and *efficient*; her bosses depend on her.

Write seven pairs of sentences (A) to identify and locate an item on Ms. Rogers's desk and (B) to comment on the item and say what it tells us about Donna Rogers.

> EXAMPLE: A. *In the middle of Donna Rogers's desk, there is a large ink blotter.*
>   B. *The blotter serves as her base of operations for running the office.*

1. _____

   _____

2. _____

   _____

3. _____

   _____

4. _____

   _____

5. _____

   _____

6. _____

   _____

7. _____

   _____

Now, rewrite your pairs of sentences as a paragraph. Begin with the introduction on page 13. Combine sentences and add transitions wherever appropriate. Also, change nouns to pronouns to avoid unnecessary repetition. Use a separate piece of paper.

Preliminary Writing

You and your teacher should decide which of the following activities to do. Write in your journal or in a special notebook.

1. Go back to Reading 1. Make a list of all the features of the glass house that appeal to you. Also make a list of the features that do *not* appeal to you.

2. You have won a lottery. The prize is your dream house! You have to design it so that the builders know what to do. Draw a sketch. Then write a description of the sketch. Also explain how you plan to furnish the house.

3. Think of places that you remember fondly. Make a list. Next to each place on your list, note two or three features that made each place attractive to you.

4. Do the same as number 3 above, except make it negative. List places that you do *not* remember fondly. Note two or three features that made each place unattractive to you.

5. Think of a public or private place you know well. Write five or six sentences about this place for each of four different visitors: an architect, an artist, a child, and an elderly person. In each set of sentences, emphasize what will appeal to the visitor.

▲ On top of the filing cabinets, there are files and a stapler.

Instructions for Composition 1

Follow these instructions as you prepare to write your own composition. Your teacher will help you understand them.

1. Choose a place that you can describe according to its physical space. As you decide, think of what you want to say through your description. For example, you might want to encourage your classmates to visit a local museum, park, or historical building by writing a self-guided tour. Emphasize what is most interesting. In other words, don't just tell where things are. Use descriptions as a means to say something more. (Check the suggested topics that follow these instructions.)

2. After you decide on your topic, make a diagram or sketch of the place you are going to describe.

3. Make some notes before you start your actual composition. Write down all the features of this place that come to mind. Decide what main point you want to make about this place. Circle the features that illustrate your main point.

4. Write your composition from your diagram/sketch and your notes. In the first paragraph, introduce your topic and then narrow down to the controlling idea of your composition. (You might actually compose the introduction *after* you write the body; that sometimes works.) In the paragraphs following the introduction, take each specific area and describe it. Then, if you need a separate conclusion, broaden back to the general topic in the last paragraph.

5. Use Reading 1 as your guide. Give your composition a title. Write on regular notebook paper and make your writing neat and attractive. Good luck!

Suggested Topics for Composition 1

Your teacher will ask you to write one or more descriptions. Use Reading 1 as your guide. Here are some suggested topics.

Composition A

Describe a room or other area that you feel positive about. If you write about a room, the room is perhaps beautiful, or it is bright and cheerful. Maybe it is only moderately pleasant, but it is very comfortable. You might have positive feelings about one of the following topics:

1. a room in your present home

2. a room in a former home

3. the office where you work or once worked

4. a room in a friend's or relative's home

5. a perfect room in a dream house

6. a park near your home

Be sure to state, as part of your controlling idea, exactly how *you* feel about the area. Then, let your description show why you feel the way you do. Give plenty of details. Plan before you write.

Composition B

Describe a place that you feel negative about. You might have many different reasons for feeling negative. Here are some possible reasons:

1. The design is cold and sterile.

2. The furnishings are old and ugly.

3. Something unpleasant happened there; you have bad memories.

4. The place is not as nice as your former place; it does not reflect you or your aspirations.

5. The place shows something negative about the person who occupies it.

Describe the place according to its arrangement of space. Let your description show what is negative. For example, you want to describe your sloppy roommate's half of the dormitory room (number 5 above). Choose details that show his/her sloppiness: *unmade bed in the corner*, *dirty clothes on the floor*, *dirty dishes on the desk*, *junk falling out of the closet*, *wastebasket overflowing on the floor*, etc. As you describe, the reader should get a mental picture of the place. Plan out your composition before you start writing.

Describe the exterior of this house. ▼

Composition C

Describe a place or an object about which you have special knowledge, possibly from research. Describe the place or object according to its spatial arrangement. If you describe an object, tell where and how the parts fit together. You might want to try one of the following topics.

1. Describe a microscope to someone who has never seen one.

2. Describe the scene of a crime to the police.

3. Describe a piece of important machinery to an engineering student.

4. Describe a building to an architecture student.

5. Describe a beautiful scene to a landscape artist.

6. Describe a moving scene to a poet.

You might need to do some research to get additional information for your composition. Add a diagram or picture to your composition if one will help the reader understand your description. Plan out your composition before you start writing.

Framing *Events* In Time

Constantine ▶

Composition Focus:	*Narration*
Organizational Focus:	*Chronological order*
Grammatical Focus:	*Past tenses*

Study the photo and pictures below. Identify Pierre Marchan in each picture and describe what you see.

- Where do you think Constantine is?
- In what military conflict do you think Pierre Marchan served?
- In what part of the world did he live out his life?

*Pierre Marchan:
The Man and His Life*

As a boy in Constantine ▲

As an army doctor ▲

With his family ▲

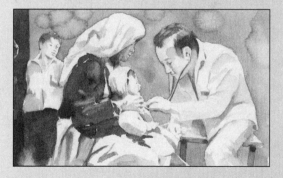

In his clinic ▲

In his sixties ▲

Just before his death ▲

PIERRE MARCHAN: THE MAN AND HIS LIFE

(1) One of the most fascinating people that I have ever known was Dr. Pierre Marchan. I first met him in Tunis, Tunisia, about twenty-five years ago. At that time, he was in his early sixties. He was a small, frail man. When he walked, he took tiny, shuffling steps. When he started to talk, however, he was transformed. His eyes would sparkle and his voice would boom. He loved to tell stories about his past, and he delighted in performing little magic tricks with cards or matches.

(2) Dr. Marchan's life was fascinating. He was born in Constantine, Algeria, the oldest child of a wealthy French couple. (See the map on page 25.) During his childhood, he was surrounded by art, literature, and music. As a young man, he wanted to become a writer, but his strong-willed father wanted him to become a medical doctor. He became a medical doctor. At the appropriate time, he married a young woman that his family had chosen for him.

(3) During World War II, Dr. Marchan saw military action in North Africa. He served as an army doctor for a division of British soldiers. Many of the stories that he later told about those days were humorous; and some were very sad. All of them made history come alive.

(4) After the war, Dr. Marchan became the village doctor in the small mining community of Djerissa on the Tunisian-Algerian border. By then, he had two children. As soon as they were old enough to go to school, they were sent to a boarding school in France. His wife left for France, too; the village was too small and poor to interest her.

(5)   Alone, Dr. Marchan worked in his clinic, delivering babies and healing the sick. During those years, he wrote some important medical books on North African diseases. These books are now on the shelves of the best medical libraries in the world. During those years, he also adopted a tiny orphan girl who became the light of his life. Some years later, the child was tragically killed in an automobile accident. He never got over her death.

(6)   The last time I saw Dr. Marchan, he looked much older and frailer. That was about three years before his death. He had had a stroke and was barely able to walk. Yet the first thing he did when we sat down together was to perform a little magic trick. That old sparkle was still there!

Author's note: Although not his real name, "Pierre Marchan" was a real person and the details here are true, according to my own experience and as told to me by Marchan. I last saw him in Tunis, Tunisia, in December, 1976; he died in Djerissa about three years later. I will always remember him fondly.

▲ Dr. Marchan and the author in Djerissa, Tunisia, in May, 1966.

Please complete the outline below with information from Reading 2. Add more numbers and letters as you need them.

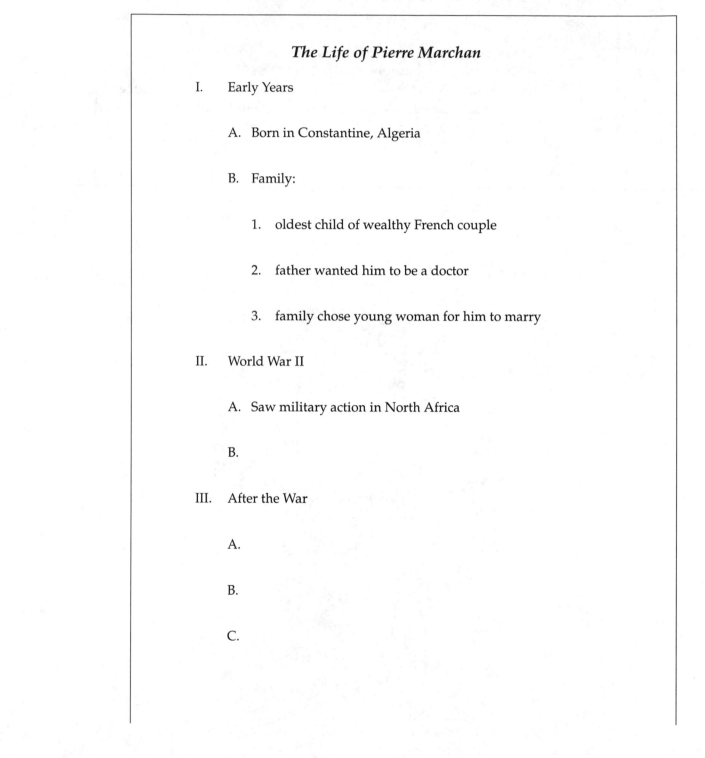

The Life of Pierre Marchan

I. Early Years

    A. Born in Constantine, Algeria

    B. Family:

        1. oldest child of wealthy French couple

        2. father wanted him to be a doctor

        3. family chose young woman for him to marry

II. World War II

    A. Saw military action in North Africa

    B.

III. After the War

    A.

    B.

    C.

IV. Living alone

    A.

    B.

    C.

V. Before his death

    A.

    B.

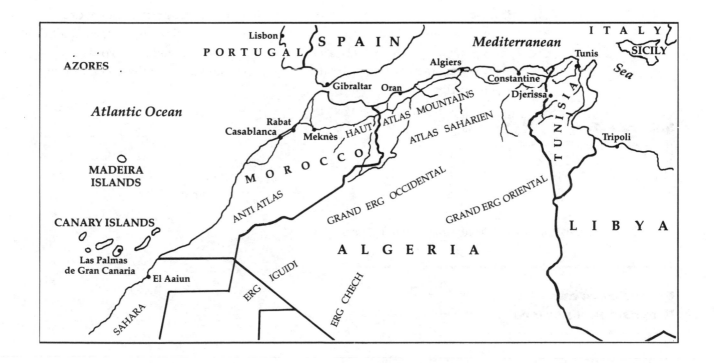

Let your teacher guide you through the following notes and questions.

1. You already know that you are writing narratively whenever you tell a story or relate events. For example, children's fairy tales are narratives; biographies and autobiographies are usually narratives; history books are partly narratives. Stories and events can be true or untrue.

   What type of narrative is Reading 2—real or fictitious? What is the approximate time frame (beginning to end)?

2. Some narratives are more formal in style than others. For example, if you wrote a letter to your cousin about your weekend camping trip, you would choose an informal style. If you were a structural engineer writing about a series of events that led to the collapse of a bridge, your style would be formal.

   What about Reading 2? How would you characterize the style?

   With your teacher, discuss what makes a narrative style more or less formal. Make a list of some narrative topics that might require different styles.

3. You already know that narratives usually follow chronological (time) order. As you can see in Reading 2, Dr. Marchan's past is divided into chronological segments. Chronological order requires you to use special time words and phrases, many of which are listed below. See how many of these you can find in Reading 2.

Subordinators

after	before	when
as soon as	until	whenever

EXAMPLE: *When he walked, he took tiny, shuffling steps.*

Prepositions and Prepositional phrases

at the (appropriate) time	during that time	on _____
by _____	during those years (months, etc.)	prior to _____
by that time	from _____ to _____	until _____
by then	from then on	upon _____
during _____	in _____	

EXAMPLE: *During his childhood, Pierre Marchan was surrounded by art, literature, and music.*

Sentence Connectors

afterwards	later (on)	subsequently
eventually	next	the first (last, etc.) time
first, second, etc.	now	then
gradually	some (months, etc.) later	years (months, days, etc.) later

EXAMPLE: *Some years later, the child was tragically killed in an automobile accident.*

Other words and phrases

ago	always	never	soon	still

EXAMPLE: *I first met him in Tunis, Tunisia, about twenty-five years ago.*

After working with these time words, take turns sharing chronological information with your teacher and classmates. For example, How old were you when you started school? Then, go on to the exercises that follow. They will help prepare you for your own writing.

Tunis, Tunisia ▼

Exercise A: Using Verb Forms

Complete the sentences below by using the appropriate forms of the verbs in parentheses. (The information is about Charles Darwin, the famous English scientist who lived from 1809 to 1882.) You will need to use each of the following forms in either the active or passive voice, at least one time.

EXAMPLE (with verb *take*):

	ACTIVE	PASSIVE
Simple present tense:	*take(s)*	*am/is/are taken*
Present perfect (simple) tense:	*has/have taken*	*has/have been taken*
Simple past tense:	*took*	*was/were taken*
Past continuous tense:	*was/were taking*	*was/were being taken*
Perfect modal form:	*would have taken*	*would have been taken*

1. Charles Darwin was one of the greatest biologists that the world *(ever see)*

   _____.

2. As a boy, Darwin thought that Latin and ancient history *(be)*

   _____ dull and useless.

3. Although his father made him study classical literature, he *(prefer)*

   _____ to study scientific subjects. (He didn't study scientific subjects.)

4. At the age of sixteen, Darwin *(send)* _____ to Scotland to study medicine.

5. Darwin *(stay)* _____ in Scotland for only two years,

   and then his father *(send)* _____ him to

   Cambridge, England, to study theology.

6. After Darwin *(graduate)* _____ from Cambridge in

    1831, he *(invite)* _____ to go on a trip around the
    world.

7. While he *(sail)* _____ around the world, his

    thoughts on evolution *(begin)* _____ to form.

8. In 1859, he *(write)* _____ his famous book, *The
    Origin of Species.*

9. Darwin's theory of evolution by natural selection *(attack)*

    _____ viciously and Darwin *(accuse)*

    _____ of destroying religion.

10. Today, Darwin's theory *(consider)* _____ to be one
    of the greatest discoveries of modern science.

Charles Darwin 1809–1882 ▶

Exercise B: Using *Would* to Signal Repeated Past Action

Part I

Write one sentence for each set below. Use *would + verb* to say that something was usual or habitual in the past. Use *and* to join the two clauses. If the two clauses have different subjects and seem long to you, put a comma before *and*.

> EXAMPLE: *When I was a child, I loved movies.*
> *I . . . go to the movies with my friends*
> *I . . . watch old movies on TV*
>
> <u>I would go to the movies with my friends and</u>
> <u>watch old movies on TV.</u>

In the second half of each sentence, don't repeat *would*; it is understood. Don't repeat the subject either, if the subject of both verbs is the same. Also, don't confuse *would* with *used to*. Both mean that something was in the past, but there is one important difference. *Used to* also means that something continuous in the past doesn't exist anymore. For example: *My brother used to smoke*.

1. When Dr. Marchan was a child, he was surrounded by art and music.
   his parents . . . take him to concerts
   he . . . visit art exhibits with his art teachers

   _____

   _____

2. When Dr. Marchan started to talk, he was transformed.
   eyes . . . sparkle
   voice . . . become strong

   _____

   _____

3. Dr. Marchan was a wonderful storyteller.
   he . . . tell about the war
   friends . . . listen in awe

   _____

   _____

4. When Charles Darwin was a boy, he was a keen observer of nature.
    he . . . wander in the woods
    he . . . spend hours examining bugs and plants

_____

_____

5. As a student, Darwin always did poorly.
    he . . . forget to do his homework
    teachers . . . scold him

_____

_____

Part II

Choose a specific period of time in your life and write five sentences about your habitual activities during that time. Use *would*. Use time expressions to indicate the time.

EXAMPLE: When I was a young child, I would spend every afternoon at my grandmother's house.

_____

_____

_____

_____

_____

_____

_____

_____

Exercise C: Emphasizing with Sentence Length

Part I

A writer can use a short sentence and a long sentence together in a very effective way. The short sentence can emphasize the consequence or aftermath of the action stated in the longer sentence.

> EXAMPLE: *My teacher told me that I had to study hard in order to pass the test.*
> I studied hard! _____

Read each sentence below and then write a very short sentence to go with it. Your sentence will say that what was expected or predicted in the first sentence actually happened.

1. Pierre Marchan's strong-willed father wanted him to become a medical

   doctor. _____

2. Charles Darwin's father firmly told him that he (Charles) was going to go to

   Scotland to study medicine. _____

3. Bill Clinton predicted that he would win the 1992 American presidential

   election. _____

4. The U.S. Geological Survey said that Mt. St. Helens would erupt in the

   spring of 1980._____

5. In 1903, Orville and Wilbur Wright argued that their airplane, the *Kitty Hawk*,

   would fly._____

Part II

Short sentences can also form pairs with longer sentences to emphasize contrast. Read the longer sentences below and follow each one with a short sentence. Let your short sentence state a contrast to what is in the longer sentence.

> EXAMPLE: *My friend promised again and again that he would come on time.*
> He didn't! _____

1. Charles Darwin's father didn't want his son to do poorly in school.

    _____

2. Pierre Marchan thought he could get over the loss of his adopted

    daughter. _____

3. Some politicians predicted that George Bush would win the 1992 American

    presidential election. _____

4. In 1980, the U.S. Geological Survey said that there would be a warning before

    the eruption of Mt. St. Helens. _____

5. In 1903, friends of Orville and Wilbur Wright said that their airplane would

    never fly. _____

Exercise D: Combining and Reducing Sentences

Write each pair of sentences below as one sentence. Reduce the second sentence by dropping the subject and the verb. Here, you can do this because both sentences name the same subject (with no object in between).

> EXAMPLE: *Charles Darwin was a famous biologist. He was the first to propose a scientific theory of evolution.*
>
> Charles Darwin was a famous biologist, the first to propose a scientific theory of evolution.

Note: This is a good way to make a double identification.

1. Charles Darwin was born in 1809. He was the son of a cultured English couple.

    _____

    _____

2. His father was a leading physician. He was a man of sharp wit and considerable personal wealth.

_____

_____

3. His mother was Susannah Darwin. She was the daughter of Josiah Wedgewood.

_____

_____

4. Charles's paternal grandfather was Erasmus Darwin. He was a man who had once refused the title of Royal Physician to King George III.

_____

_____

5. Charles's maternal grandfather was Josiah Wedgewood. Wedgewood was a maker of fine china.

_____

_____

Charles Darwin's boat, *The Beagle* ▲

Exercise E: Using Time Expressions

Choose expressions from the following list to complete the text below:

as a boy　　　　　　　　　　　　*during the voyage*
at that time　　　　　　　　　　　*in 1825*
at the appropriate age　　　　　　*in 1859*
by then　　　　　　　　　　　　　*in those days*
during his Cambridge years　　　　*today*
　　　　　　　　　　　　　　　　　upon graduation

Use each expression only once. Read the entire text before you start. Then work in small groups to fill in the blanks.

CHARLES DARWIN

One of the greatest biologists the world has ever seen was Charles Darwin. Darwin was born in Shrewsbury, England, in February, 1809. (1) _____ , Shrewsbury was a busy market town surrounded by rich farmlands. Darwin was born to a cultured middle-class family. His father was the leading physician of the town; his mother was the daughter of Josiah Wedgewood, a maker of fine china.

(2) _____ , Darwin showed a keen interest in living things. He loved to wander in the woods looking at plants and birds. (3) _____ , he was enrolled in the Shrewsbury School. There he studied Latin, classical literature, and ancient history. Young Charles thought that these subjects were dull and useless; he would have preferred scientific studies. As a result, he did poorly. In fact, his grades were so low that his father thought he was a disgrace to the family.

(4) _____ , at the age of sixteen, Darwin was sent to Scotland to study medicine. He studied there for two years and continued to do poorly. At one point, he wrote to his sister that his medical courses were utterly *stupid*. (5) _____ , Darwin's father knew that his son would never become a doctor.

Darwin's father then sent him to Cambridge to become a clergyman. (6) _____ , Darwin had a passion for collecting beetles, but to him it was only a hobby. He didn't take it seriously. One person at Cambridge, however, did. That was Professor John Henslow, the head of the botany department.

Somehow, Darwin managed to graduate from Cambridge in 1831. (7) _____ , Professor Henslow arranged for him to accompany a certain Captain Fitzroy on a survey trip around the world. (8) _____ , Darwin collected rocks, bones, and insects. He made extensive notes on all that he observed. The thoughts that led to his theory of evolution were beginning to form.

The widely accepted theory (9) _____ _____ was that God created each creature separately and individually. (10) _____ , Darwin published his famous book, *The Origin of Species*. In it, he explained his theory of evolution by natural selection. The theory was instantly and viciously attacked. Darwin was accused of destroying religion and insulting the human race. (11) _____ , however, Darwin's theory is considered to be one of the greatest discoveries of modern science.

Preliminary Writing

You and your teacher should decide which of the following activities to do. Write in your journal or in a special notebook.

1. Go back to Reading 2. Read through it again. Then close your book and make a list from memory of the details of Dr. Marchan's life. Don't worry if you forget some details.

2. Make a list of the remarkable individuals that you have known. Choose only ones that you have known well or that you know a lot about. Beside each name on your list, note three or four details about each person.

3. Make a list of periods of time in your life when significant changes occurred. Beside each period of time, note details of these changes.

4. Choose one of the individuals from your list (number 2 above). Write three short pieces about the person, each for a different purpose. Write one introducing him or her to a friend; another recommending him or her for a job; and a third as an obituary to be placed in a newspaper.

Instructions for Composition 2

Follow the instructions below as you prepare to write.

1. Choose a topic that you can develop according to time; in other words, organize your material chronologically. For example, you might relate the sequence of political events in a recent revolution, you may want to discuss the migration of a group of refugees from one part of the world to another, or you might want to tell about a person whose life and work have influenced your education. (See a list of suggested topics in the following section.)

2. Whether you write about events, people, or both, think about your role in the narrative. Are you an outside observer or a participant? Make your role clear. If you do not understand the difference between observer and participant, go back to the beginning of Unit 2. Read the text on Marchan (Reading 2) and the text on Darwin (Exercise E). In the beginning and end, the writer of Reading 2 is part of the narrative, but the writer of the Darwin text is an outside person.

3. As you choose your topic, think about what you want to show through your narrative. For example, the writer of Reading 2 wants to show how fascinating Pierre Marchan was—the events in his life, his happiness and his sadness.

4. After you decide on your topic, jot down all that comes to mind about it. Read over your notes; circle those details that illustrate and explain what you want to show.

5. Write a draft of your composition. Use Reading 2 as your guide. Read through your writing and make sure that it says what you want to say. Make changes where you want.

6. Give your composition a title and write on 8 ½ x 11 inch notebook paper. Leave wide, clean margins and indent each paragraph. Add pictures, a time line, or whatever will help your reader follow your writing.

Suggested Topics for Composition 2

Your teacher will ask you to write one or more narrative compositions following the instructions already given. Here are some suggested topics.

Composition A

Tell about the life of a person who is memorable or important to you. The person may be dead or alive. Your composition might need to cover only a certain period of the person's life. Use the details of the person's life to say something about the person or about your relationship to the person. Here are some possible topics:

1. a person who has influenced your ideas and your education

2. a person who once saved your life in some way

3. a person who helped raise you

4. the most fascinating or unusual person you have ever known

5. the most unpleasant person you have ever known

6. a person who has shown great strength and courage

In your introduction, be sure to state your connection to the person—if you are a participant in the narrative. Also, say what the details of the person's life show.

Composition B

Tell about a period of time or series of events that were important in your life. Limit the time; don't tell about your whole life! The time and events may be recent or part of the distant past. Compositions A and B will both be narratives, but in B the period of time or the events—not people—are the focus of your writing. Here are some possible topics:

1. an important moment in your childhood

2. a period of great change in your life

3. a memorable experience, such as a wedding, a birth, a graduation

4. a traumatic experience, such as an accident, a death, a time of war or revolution

5. a moment of great insight or understanding

6. a humorous experience

Use the details of what happened to make a point. For example, you might want to show how a tragic fire helped you understand for the first time (number 5 above) something your parents had always tried to teach you—that people are more important than possessions.

Composition C

Relate a series of events about which you have special knowledge, probably from research. Here are some possibilities:

1. Relate the eruption of Mount Pinatubo in the Philippines. (See newspapers of June 9, 10, and 11, 1991.)

2. Briefly narrate the development of the airplane—from the *Kitty Hawk* to the *Concorde* and beyond. (Check an encyclopedia or a book on aviation history.)

3. Narrate the life of a famous scientist, such as Galileo Galilei, Isaac Newton, or Albert Einstein. (Check an encyclopedia for dates and other details.)

4. Trace the migration of Cambodian or Vietnamese refugees from Southeast Asia to the West. (Use your personal knowledge, or the knowledge of classmates; also check the *Reader's Guide to Periodical Literature* for recent publications. The *Reader's Guide* is a listing of magazines and newspapers organized by title and subject. It can be found in your library.)

Add a chart, map, or time line to your composition, if one will help your reader(s) follow your narrative.

Analyzing
Patterns

▲ relationship ▼

◄ place ▲

Composition Focus:	*Analysis*
Organizational Focus:	*Partition*
Grammatical Focus:	*Clauses*

Study the photos.

- What is the general idea?
- What do you see in each pair of photos?
- What differences do you see among the three pairs of photos and between the two photos of each pair?
- Can you think of other factors that affect how people speak English?
- Can you think of other factors that affect how people speak *your* native language?

▲ purpose ▶

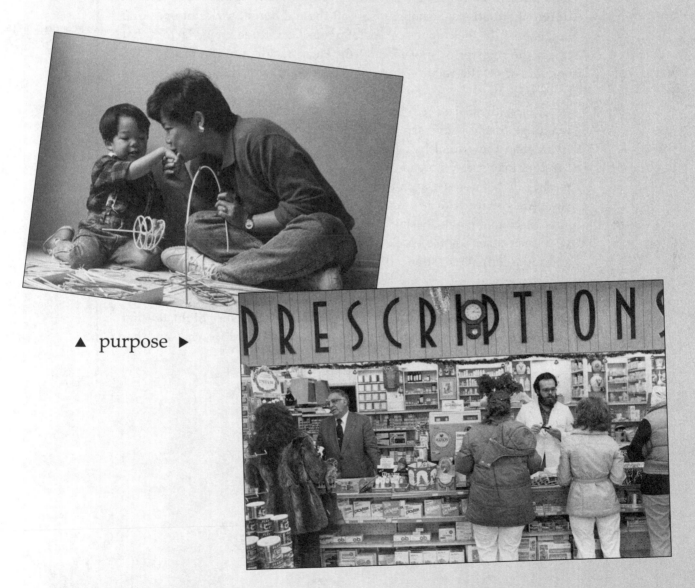

Factors Affecting
Spoken English

"I Beg Your Pardon"

(1) **L**earning to understand spoken English can be difficult. The learner must master new sounds, stress and intonation patterns, and conversational idioms. That seems hard enough, but learners soon realize that there is something else going on to block their comprehension: speakers *change* their speech. In other words, the very same speaker speaks differently in different situations. Sociolinguists call these different styles of speaking "registers." In their analyses, sociolinguists cite three major factors that affect the register of spoken English. These factors are the place of the conversation, the relationship of the speakers, and the purpose of the conversation.

(2) First, the place where the conversation takes place directly affects the language of the conversation. People generally speak more formally at work than they do at home. Even two best friends who work and live together may speak more formally to each other in the office. At home, one might say, "C'mon, I wanna leave," while the same person at work might say, "Are you ready to go now?"

Second, the relationship of the speakers affects the language they use with each other. People speak more casually to friends and acquaintances and more formally to strangers. Because we already share information and experience with friends and acquaintances, we do not need to explain as much. People who know each other well might use more idioms and more slang in their speech. If a person were very angry, she might tell her daughter to "hush her mouth," her mother to "quiet down," and her secretary to "refrain from yelling."

(3)　　　　Finally, the purpose of the conversation affects people's speech. A person who wants to analyze a problem might speak about "factors," "reasons," and "solutions." A person who wants to complain might ask a lot of "why" questions ("Why do I have to work late again?") and make negative statements ("You never listen to me when I'm talking to you"). A person who wants to soothe hurt feelings uses a quiet, soothing tone, while a person who wants to pick a fight speaks rapidly and loudly, using words like "chicken" and "stupid" and may curse a lot.

(4)　　　　Few speakers realize that they change registers according to these factors; in fact, most people would strongly deny it. These changes are subconscious and automatic for all of us. We accept the changeability of the weather, but we often refuse to accept the changeability of speech.

Author's note: If you are interested in the topic of conversational styles, I encourage you to read a little book by Martin Joos entitled *The Five Clocks* (New York: Harcourt Brace, 1967). You might also enjoy Deborah Tannen's *That's Not What I Meant* (New York: Ballantine Books, 1986), and *You Just Don't Understand* (New York: Ballantine Books, 1991) on the differences between men's and women's conversational styles. Check your school library for these books.

▲ What speaking "register" do you think the people in the photograph are using?

Please complete the outline below with information from Reading 3. Add numbers and letters where necessary.

Factors Affecting Spoken English

I. Place of conversation

    A.

        1.

        2.

II. Relationship of the speakers to each other

III.

Let your teacher guide you through the following notes and questions.

1. When you analyze, you look for a pattern of related parts that fit together to form a whole. These parts are not physical ones. Rather, they are mental divisions that help to answer the questions *what*, *how*, or *why*. For example, *what factors contribute to heart disease? Why do some people, and not others, get heart disease? What are the consequences of heart disease?* These are all questions that require analysis.

   In Reading 3, what question is answered?

   You can already see that the divisions must be related in order for your analysis to make sense. Analyses often examine the following:

types or kinds	problems
factors	causes
uses	qualities or characteristics
reasons	effects or consequences
ways	

   In Reading 3, what is the nature of the analysis? In other words, what does the writer examine?

2. Let's focus for a moment on when and where your analysis takes place. The divisions are mental; this means that you have to make the analysis in your own head. This unit of the textbook will show you how a writer of English puts together an analytic composition, but you have to do your mental analysis before you can start to put together your composition. Analyzing takes a lot of mental work. It requires a quick, resourceful mind.

3. Let's see what you need in your written analysis. You have to tell the reader the following:

   a. your general topic
   b. any subtopics of the general topic
   c. your method of analyzing (e.g., *uses, causes, ways*)
   d. how many divisions you have
   e. what those divisions are
   f. examples or details of each division

   Go back to Reading 3 and identify all of these components. Where do you find each of them?

4. In the introduction, writers usually state the topic, a possible subtopic, the method and the number of divisions. The writer of Reading 3 names the divisions (here, the *factors*) at the beginning and then states each one again in the body. Writers sometimes wait until they get to the body to name each division. You can do it either way.

   How does the writer of Reading 3 signal the movement from one factor to another factor? Are the three factors in Reading 3 of equal importance? Does it matter which one is first, which is second, etc.?

   Writers will sometimes rank their divisions: perhaps some are more important than others.

5. Look at the details that support each factor in Reading 3. Look at the first factor. What kind of details supports it? What is the relationship between the supporting sentences?

   Look at the second factor. Does the writer give the same kind of support? What is the relationship between the supporting sentences?

   Look at the third factor. Are the details of the same kind? Is the relationship between the supporting sentences the same or different?

Before going on to the exercises, take turns sharing experiences that relate to Reading 3. Have you noticed the kinds of changes discussed in the reading? When? Where? What difficulties do you have understanding spoken English? Analyze these difficulties with your classmates. Have you noticed differences not discussed in the reading? Dialect differences, perhaps?

Exercise A: Using Quotation Marks

As you can see in Reading 3, you need to use quotation marks in your writing to enclose the following:

1. the exact words of a speaker:

   EXAMPLE: *"I'll think it over," he responded.*

2. the title of a story (not a book), article, chapter, song, or short poem:

   EXAMPLE: *You should read "Marrakech," by George Orwell.*

3. a word or phrase that you want to define, explain, or call attention to:

   EXAMPLE: *I asked my teacher the meaning of the word "factor."*

Note that end punctuation (a comma, period, question mark, or exclamation mark) is usually *inside* the closing quotation marks. Also, in some places where you might use quotation marks, printers of books use *italics*.

In the texts below, add quotation marks wherever you think they are needed. You do not need to rewrite.

Text A: Wrong Bus, Lady!

People sometimes express their irritation in indirect ways. An experience I had on a city bus the other day is a good example.

I got on one bus while thinking I was on another one. When I realized I was on the wrong bus, I said to the driver, Pardon me, but I think I'm lost. Could you tell me where you're going?

The driver looked at me for a moment and then replied, I go lots of places, lady. Where are *you* going?

Text B: Mr. Jones, or is it Paul?

Americans seem very informal with each other, but they do observe some important social conventions. One of these conventions concerns the use of first names. An older neighbor, for example, should be called Mr. Jones, unless he has given his younger neighbors permission to call him Paul. A client should be called Ms. McCall, until she asks her insurance agent to call her Betty. If the first name is used too soon, it can make one person feel that the other is disrespectful.

Text C: Dear Petunia

Humor can result from the use of formal speech where informal speech is expected. There are wonderful examples in children's books. In a popular book entitled Petunia, I Love You, Racoon, a very hungry creature, tries to trick Petunia, a fat and juicy goose, away from the safe barnyard.

It would make me so happy just to have your company for a little walk in the forest, said Racoon.

You are so polite and kind, Racoon, said Petunia. It would be rude of me to refuse. Pray, lead the way.

To you the honor, dear Petunia. I'll walk behind you, replied Racoon.

(Taken from *Petunia, I Love You*, by Roger Duvoisin. New York: Alfred A. Knopf, 1965)

Exercise B: Using Sentences of Partition

Part I

Use words from the following list to complete the first sentence of each group below:

> *types*   *uses*   *ways*
>
> *factors*   *reasons*   *causes*

Caution: You will need to use some words more than once. Also, you will need to read all of the sentences in each group in order to know how to fill in the blank.

> EXAMPLE: *Linguists cite three major* ___factors___ *that affect the register of spoken English. They are the place where a person is speaking, the people that a person is speaking to, and the purpose of the conversation.*

1. There are three major _____ in which vitamins are lost from food. They dissolve in water, they are changed by heat, and the part of the plant containing the vitamin is thrown away.

2. Sports are of two basic _____ . There are those that are played by teams, and those that are played by individuals.

3. There are three major _____ why more and more areas of the world are becoming desert. Farmers are overgrazing, cutting down trees and bushes for firewood, and overplanting.

4. A razor blade has three main _____ . It is used for shaving, of course, but it can also be used for fine cutting and scraping.

5. According to medical doctors, there are two immediate

   _____ of heart disease. One is arteriosclerosis, or hardening of the arteries; the other is the buildup of cholesterol in the arteries leading to the heart.

6. There are five important _____ which may speed up the process of heart disease. They are poor diet, cigarette smoking, lack of exercise, excess weight, and high blood pressure.

7. According to law enforcement authorities, banks actually help robbers in

   three _____ . First, banks do not properly teach
   employees what to do in case of robbery. Second, they do not maintain
   cameras and silent alarms. Third, they are more concerned with the
   appearance of the bank than its security.

8. There are three fundamental _____ why our bodies
   need water to stay healthy. First, water helps to control the temperature of
   the body. Second, it promotes all bodily processes, such as digestion. Finally,
   water cleans the tissues.

Part II

Change the Type A sentences below to Type B sentences according to the
examples given. The sentences that you write in this exercise would probably
appear in the introduction of a composition.

> EXAMPLE: **A.** *There are several important ways in which the weather affects our lives.*
> **B.** *The weather affects our lives in several important ways.*

1. **A.** There are three major ways in which vitamins are lost from food.

   B. _____

2. **A.** There are several fundamental ways in which leaves benefit the earth.

   B. _____

3. **A.** There are three important ways in which banks help robbers.

   B. _____

4. **A.** There are several basic ways in which the quality of urban life is declining.

   B. _____

5. **A.** There are several fundamental ways in which the earth is becoming
   increasingly polluted.

   B. _____

   _____

Exercise C: Using Gerunds

Answer each question below by using the information that is given. The grammar of the question will require you to change verbs to gerunds *(verb + -ING)*.

> EXAMPLE: Information: *It is difficult to learn to understand spoken English.*
> Question: *What is difficult?*
>
> Answer: Learning to understand spoken English
> is difficult.

1. Information: It is important to follow social conventions in a new culture.
   Question: What is important?

   _____

2. Information: Writers can create humor when they exaggerate formal speech.
   Question: What writing technique can create humor?

   _____

3. Information: It is important for banks to teach employees what to do in case of robbery. This will help to improve bank security.
   Question: What will help to improve bank security?

   _____

4. Information: Banks can install cameras and silent alarms in order to help improve security.
   Question: What will also help to improve bank security?

   _____

5. Information: One of the goals of modern medicine is to discover a cure for cancer.
   Question: What is one of the goals of modern medicine?

   _____

Exercise D: Writing with Clauses

Part I

You probably already know how to write sentences with adjective clauses such as these:

> A person **who likes classical music** will surely want to get a season ticket to the symphony.
> This is the book **that you asked me to get from the library.**

You can use either *who* or *that* to refer to people and *that* or *which* to refer to things or animals. However, if you begin your adjective clause with a preposition, use *preposition + which* (for things or animals) or *preposition + whom* (for people).

> EXAMPLE: *The man for whom I did the work paid me well.*
> *The school to which you applied offers a number of valuable programs.*

In the exercise below, change the second sentence of each pair into a dependent clause and add it to the first. You will need a clause marker: *that, which,* or *who.*

1. Scientists cite three major ways. Vitamins are lost from our food in these

   ways. _____

   _____

2. Botanists tell us of several fundamental ways. Leaves benefit the earth in

   these ways. _____

   _____

3. Medical doctors cite five factors. These factors speed up heart disease.

   _____

   _____

4. Educators believe that there are environmental factors. These can affect a

   child's ability to learn. _____

   _____

5. Banks improve their own security. They teach their employees what to do in case of robbery. (Careful!) _____

_____

Part II

Complete each sentence with a dependent clause.

1. I am a person _____

2. English is a language _____

_____

3. People _____

_____ are more likely to get heart disease.

4. An ideal teacher is one _____

_____

5. The sports _____ are hockey and soccer.

Exercise E: Supporting with Specifics

Part I

When you write in English, you have to move up and down levels of generality.

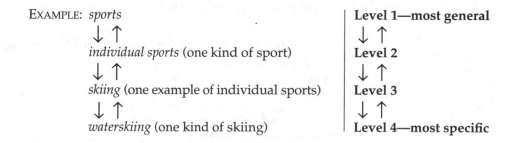

EXAMPLE: *sports*   **Level 1—most general**
↓ ↑   ↓ ↑
individual sports (one kind of sport)   **Level 2**
↓ ↑   ↓ ↑
skiing (one example of individual sports) **Level 3**
↓ ↑   ↓ ↑
waterskiing (one kind of skiing)   **Level 4—most specific**

When you write an analysis, you must operate on at least two levels: a general level that covers the whole topic and a more specific level that gives divisions of the general level.

In the following example, there are two levels: one whole (general) and two equal parts (specific).

EXAMPLE: *I have set several important future goals for myself. First, I want to master English in order to complete my education. Second, I want to get a good job so that I can support my family.*

general:
future goals
specific 1:
English for education
specific 2:
job to support family

In the exercise below, write two sentences to complete each short text. In your sentences, name some specifics of the topic introduced by the general beginning sentence. Express your own knowledge and experience in the specifics.

Text A: Learning English

There are several linguistic factors that make it difficult for a foreign student to learn English.

First,_____

_____

_____

Second,_____

_____

_____

Text B: Adjusting to a New Country

It is difficult for foreign students to adjust to life in a new country for several reasons.

First,_____

_____

_____

Second,_____

_____

_____

Text C: Adjusting to Marriage

     There are a number of important adjustments that people must make when they get married.

First,_____

_____

_____

Second,_____

_____

_____

Part II

The sample text below contains three levels of generalization. Read it several times to be sure you see the different levels.

My Ideal Husband

EXAMPLE TEXT:	*My ideal husband would have to have several important qualities.*	**whole (general)**
	First, he would be kind and loving. For example, he would never stay angry for long and he would always find little ways to make life more fun for his family.	**specific 1** **examples (of 1)**
	Second, he would be willing to share in the responsibilities of the household. He would, for instance, do some of the cooking, laundry, and cleaning. He would also share in the raising of our children.	**specific 2** **examples (of 2)**
	Finally, he would be handsome. He would be tall and thin with straight teeth and dark eyes.	**specific 3** **examples (of 3)**

Complete the following text by writing two examples (in complete sentences) for each specific part. The notes in italics may help you. Use the following phrases to signal your examples:

for example   *for instance*
to illustrate

English: An International Language

English has become an important international language. First, it is important in international communication.

    EXAMPLES: *airline pilots*
                   TV news
                   international newspapers

_____

_____

_____

_____

_____

Second, English is important in business and commerce.

    EXAMPLES: *World Bank*
                   Common Market
                   trade negotiations
                   international currency exchange

_____

_____

_____

_____

_____

Finally, English is important in international relations.

    EXAMPLES: *United Nations*
                   World Court
                   international treaties
                   diplomatic arrangements
                   Organization of American States

_____

_____

_____

_____

_____

Preliminary Writing

You and your teacher can decide which of the following activities to do. Write in your journal or in a special notebook.

1. Make a list of the qualities of an ideal spouse, an ideal parent, or an ideal teacher. Make your list as long as possible. Analyze qualities on your list and group them into *types* of qualities, if possible. Give each type a label if you can.

2. Write about how you change your speech in your native language. How do you speak to someone older than you? Younger than you? How do you speak to someone in a position of authority? etc. Analyze these differences.

3. Write a brief paragraph about why you are studying English. Give details whenever possible.

4. Briefly analyze the consequences of an important event or decision in your life. What has happened as a result? Give details. Did the event or decision turn out to be positive or negative?

5. Think of a particular situation or circumstance that happened in your family. Analyze it from the perspective of at least two different people. For example, did it affect you and one of your siblings or you and your parents differently?

Instructions for Composition 3

Follow the instructions below as you prepare to write your composition.

1. Choose a topic that you can analyze, or choose a particular aspect of a topic to analyze. For example, A) *the institution of marriage* would be too broad a topic to analyze, but B) *adjustments to marriage* might make a good subject. (Check the suggested topics that follow.)

2. Decide how to approach your topic. In other words, think it through. For example, if you analyzed (B) above, you would have to decide on your particular focus—types of adjustments, consequences of adjustments, problems in adjusting, the very nature of the adjustments themselves, etc. You might mentally have to run through several different analyses before you find one that you can complete. Make notes as you think.

3. Be sure that you clearly state the topic (and possibly the subtopic) of your analysis, your method of analysis, the number of divisions, and the names of the divisions. Also, think of examples or other details that will help make the divisions clear to the reader.

4. Make a list of details that come to mind as you think about your topic. Organize your list: See where the details fit into groups. Draw arrows or put circles around those that belong together.

5. Write a draft of your composition, working from your list and notes. Read and reread it to be sure that it says what you want to say. Make changes as you go. Refer to Reading 3 if you need to borrow ideas, vocabulary, or grammatical structures.

6. Give your composition a title. Write on 8 ½ x 11 inch notebook paper. Leave wide, clear margins and indent each paragraph.

▲ What type of English do you think this public speaker is using? Casual? Formal?

Suggested Topics for Composition 3

Your teacher will ask you to write one or more analytic compositions. Here are some suggested topics.

Composition A

Analyze a topic of personal concern to you. It might be a matter that you have already thought a lot about, or one that you want to think about. Give it some serious thought and let your writing reflect that thought. Here are some possibilities:

1. Analyze the qualities of an ideal person: an ideal spouse (husband or wife), an ideal parent (mother or father), an ideal student or teacher, an ideal employer or employee. Either your sentences need to be hypothetical (present-unreal) with *would, should, might,* or *could* (see the sample text in Ex. E II on p. 55), or you must create a present-real situation. (Perhaps you can paint a picture of your ideal ___X___ , e.g., "I have a picture in my mind of my ideal husband. He is tall and handsome . . . .")

2. Analyze the qualities that you try to have now (whether or not you succeed), or the qualities that you hope you will have as a spouse, parent, employer or employee, student or professional person. Think of grammatical constructions that will be helpful. For example, in present time, you might need *I try to be* . . ., *I wish (that) I were.* . . . In future time, you might need *I will try to be* . . ., *I hope (that) I will.* . . .

3. Analyze your short-term or long-term goals. What are they? Why are they your goals? What will you do when you achieve your goals? What will you do if you don't achieve your goals? You may need some of the following constructions:

   I plan to (verb)   *I hope to (verb)*
   I plan on (verb + ing)   *I want to (verb)*
   I will try to (verb)   *I hope to be able to (verb)*

Composition B

Analyze a topic that is not personal, but one that requires you to use some personal knowledge and experience. Here are some choices:

1. Analyze the kinds of decisions that must be made by a teenager entering adulthood. For example, a teenager must make career decisions. Give details.

2. Analyze the kinds of adjustments that a newly married person must make. What are the major adjustments? Can they be grouped analytically? For example, are there professional adjustments, social adjustments, personal adjustments, emotional adjustments, etc.? Give examples.

3. Analyze the problems faced by a foreigner in a new country. Perhaps the newcomer is alone or with a family. Perhaps the person has come to study temporarily or settle permanently. What are the different types of problems—economic, linguistic, etc.? Give illustrations.

Composition C

Analyze a topic about which you have special knowledge. You may need to do research in order to get enough information for an analysis. Here are some possibilities:

1. Analyze the contributions to modern science of a famous scientist, such as Galileo Galilei, Isaac Newton, Charles Darwin, or Albert Einstein. (Check an encyclopedia for dates and other details.)

2. Briefly analyze the political situation in the country of your choice. (Check the *Reader's Guide* in the library for recent publications.)

3. Analyze the types of social problems facing a certain country or group of people. (Check the *Reader's Guide* in the library for recent publications.)

Practice Composition Exam: A

In order to get you accustomed to taking a composition exam, your teacher may want you to take a practice writing test from time to time. Pretend now that this is a real test. You have _____ minutes to write your exam. You may (not) use a dictionary. Follow your teacher's special instructions. Your teacher will probably want you to write only one composition.

Exam A1: Write a narrative composition on one of the following:
    a. the worst day of your life
    b. the most exciting thing that has ever happened to you
    c. the most exasperating person that you have ever known
    d. a topic chosen by you or your teacher

Exam A2: Write a physical description of one of the following:
    a. the most interesting structure on campus
    b. the most useful appliance on the market
    c. the most unusual design in nature (example: a giraffe, a waterfall, a willow tree)
    d. a topic chosen by you or your teacher

Exam A3: Write an analysis of one of the following:
    a. an event in the news
    b. culture shock
    c. changes in women's roles in a particular country
    d. a topic chosen by you or your teacher

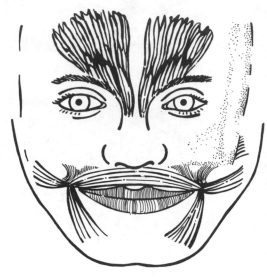

Diagram A: Our facial muscles move when ▲ we smile and laugh.

Making *Meaning* Clear

Composition Focus:	*Definition*
Organizational Focus:	*Partition*
Grammatical Focus:	*Nouns*

Study the photo and illustrations. Describe what you see in each one.

- Where are the facial muscles located—specifically?
- Where are the white blood cells?
- Why are certain parts of the body identified in diagram C?
- How do all of the diagrams connect to "laughter"?
- What do you expect to read about in Reading 4?

Diagram B: Laughter may help our white blood cells produce antibodies to fight infection. ▼

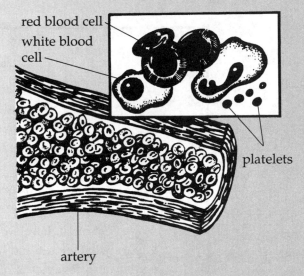

red blood cell
white blood cell
platelets
artery

Diagram C: Laughter gives the diaphragm, abdomen, heart, lungs, and liver a thorough massage. It also causes the adrenal glands to produce adrenaline. ▼

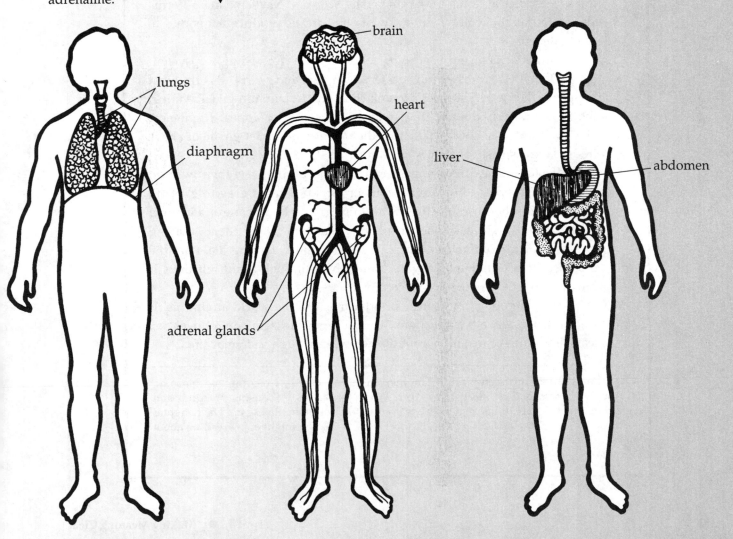

lungs

diaphragm

adrenal glands

brain

heart

liver

abdomen

LAUGHTER

(1) Some people giggle quietly. Others let loose with hearty laughter, sometimes called a "belly" laugh. However we laugh, laughter is a necessary ingredient of a healthy, happy life. We can easily recognize laughter, but what exactly is it?

(2) First of all, laughter is a physiological expression. This expression is, in part, what we see and hear. According to medical researchers, laughter is a series of movements of the facial muscles and the respiratory system. These movements give the diaphragm, abdomen, heart, lungs, and liver a thorough massage during a hearty laugh. They also cause the production of adrenaline and increase the flow of blood to the heart and brain. The results are a feeling of pleasure and well-being.

(3) It is also possible that laughter bolsters our bodies' defenses against disease. Studies at Loma Linda University School of Medicine in California show that laughter may help our white blood cells produce antibodies to fight infection.

(4) Laughter is also a psychological expression. According to psychologists, laughter expresses our mastery over fear and worry. Picture what happens when a parent takes a young child into a swimming pool. At first, the child probably doesn't laugh and may even cry or appear frightened. However, once the child is sure that the parent will not let go, he or she is free to laugh, splash, and enjoy the water.

(5) If laughter expresses mastery over fear and worry, then why do people laugh when they are nervous or afraid? That is easy to explain. People laugh then because they want to *pretend* to be in control. Picture a student who laughs easily before a big examination. The student is saying to herself or himself and to others, "See, this isn't bothering me. I am the master of this situation." Laughter can help us through a difficult time. It can actually give us time to gain control.

(6) Laughter, then, measures our adjustment to the world around us. If we can laugh when we are afraid, we will be able to gain control over our fears; if we are secure and in control, then we can laugh and enjoy life.

Author's note: On the subject of laughter and good health, I recommend Norman Cousins's *Anatomy of an Illness* (New York: W.W. Norton, 1979). Cousins, an editor and writer, also talks about his own recovery from a life-threatening illness in "The Laughter Prescription," *Saturday Evening Post*, October 1990, p. 34. You might enjoy reading about his experience.

Taking Notes

Reread Reading 4. Then, try to complete the information below from memory. If you have trouble, look back.

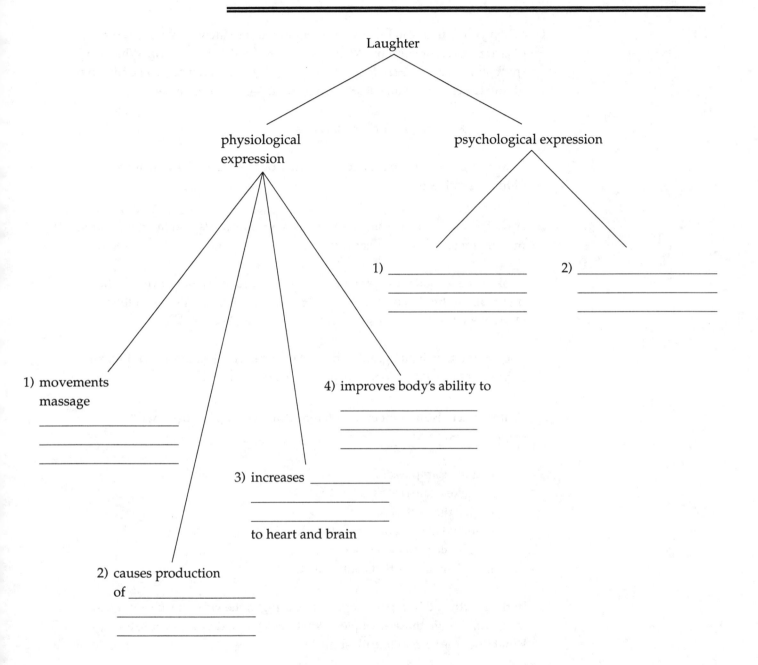

Laughter

physiological expression

psychological expression

1) _____
_____
_____

2) _____
_____
_____

1) movements massage
_____
_____
_____

4) improves body's ability to
_____
_____
_____

3) increases _____
_____
_____
to heart and brain

2) causes production
of _____
_____
_____

Notes and Questions on Reading 4

Let your teacher guide you through the following notes and questions.

1. When you define, you identify. You might want to identify a person, place, object, process, or concept. What is an *astronaut*? What is a *porch*? What is a *spark plug*? What is *electrolysis*? What is *happiness*? As a writer, you define by giving the category and special characteristics of X (your subject):

    X = category + characteristics

    In Reading 4, what subject does the writer define? How does the writer define the subject?

2. A writer can define in a single sentence; a writer can also extend a definition over many sentences and paragraphs.

    Look at the second paragraph of Reading 4. Here the writer develops the first major definition of *laughter*. Try to condense it into a single sentence (X = category + characteristics). Your sentence will be long!

    Look at the fourth paragraph. There, the writer develops the second major definition of *laughter*. Condense it into a single sentence.

3. Writers often use a number of different strategies to help them write extended definitions:

    a. give examples of X
    b. make analogies (*X is like Y*)
    c. give the uses of X
    d. tell what X is not (a negative definition)
    e. give more characteristics of X
    f. explain factors that contribute to X

    In the fourth and fifth paragraphs of Reading 4, the writer uses examples (*a* above). Locate those examples. What does the first example illustrate? What does the second one illustrate?

    In the fifth paragraph, the writer explains some contributing factors (*f* above). Study the fifth paragraph to see how it fits into the writer's development of Reading 4. What idea presented earlier does it extend? (In the same way, what idea does the third paragraph extend?)

4. The conclusion of Reading 4 is a summary. What is left out? Why do you think the writer left part of the text out of the summary?

Before going on to the exercises, discuss your ideas about laughter with your classmates. Do the ideas in Reading 4 seem true to you? Do you laugh when you are nervous or afraid? Have you noticed any differences between your culture and others regarding when and how people laugh?

Exercise A: Practicing Subject-Verb Agreement

Complete each sentence below with the appropriate form of the verb in parentheses. All verbs will be in the simple present tense; you only have to decide if the verb form is third-person singular or not. In long, complex sentences, identify the subject of the verb first.

> EXAMPLE: *Laughter (be)* _____is_____ *a psychological phenomenon*
> *that (express)* __expresses__ *our mastery over fear and*
> *worry.*

1. One of the most pleasant sounds in the world *(be)* _____ the laughter of a small child.

2. Research *(show)* _____ that there *(be)* _____ two immediate causes of heart failure.

3. Love *(be)* _____ a deep emotional bond between two people

who *(like)* _____ and *(respect)* _____ each other.

4. Engineering and computer science *(be)* _____ two fields of

study that foreign students often *(pursue)* _____ .

5. Laughter *(be)* _____ a series of movements of the facial

muscles and respiratory system which *(cause)* _____ the
production of adrenaline.

6. Medical research *(tell)* _____ us that night blindness, an eye

disorder, and rickets, a bone disease, both *(result)* _____ from
vitamin deficiencies.

7. Mathematics and linguistics (be) _____ both important fields of

study, but linguistics (be) _____ more interesting to me.

8. The place where a conversation (take) _____ place (affect)

_____ the formality of the speech.

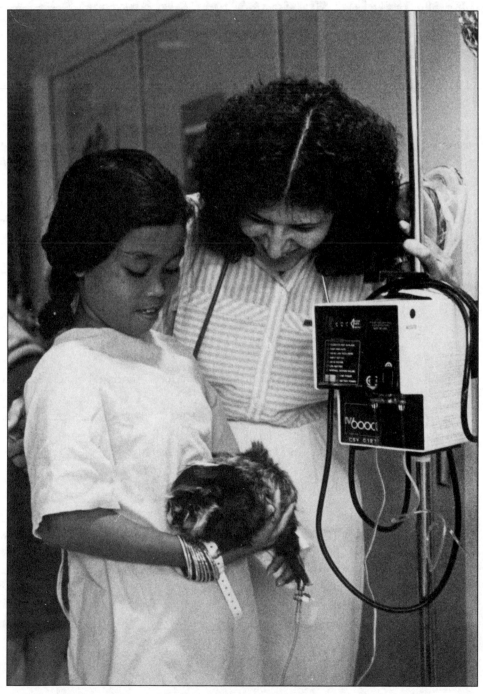

▲ A hospitalized girl is cheered up by a visit from her pet.

Exercise B: Shifting from Verbs to Nouns

The following questions ask you to identify phenomena or people. Answer each question by drawing information from the sentence above it. Change key verbs to nouns. You will also need to use the word *of*.

> EXAMPLE: *When we laugh, we express our mastery over fear and worry.*
> Question: *What is laughter?*
> Laughter is an expression of mastery over fear and worry.

1. Pierre Marchan mastered little magic tricks with cards and matches.
    Question: Who was Pierre Marchan?

    _____

    _____

2. When we laugh, we move our facial muscles and respiratory system.
    Question: What is *laughter*?

    _____

    _____

3. As a boy, Charles Darwin observed nature.
    Question: Who was Charles Darwin?

    _____

    _____

4. Socrates taught philosophy to young Greeks in the fifth century B.C.
    Question: Who was Socrates?

    _____

    _____

5. In the nineteenth century, Ludwig van Beethoven, a German, composed symphonic masterpieces.
    Question: Who was Beethoven?

    _____

    _____

6. When the earth moves because of pressures far below its surface, we call that an *earthquake*.
Question: What are *earthquakes*?

_____

_____

7. When we laugh, we express happiness.
Question: What is *laughter*?

_____

_____

Exercise C: Writing Definitions

As you know, a formal definition has three components:

A ⟶	B ⟶	C
X . . . what is being defined $=$	CATEGORY that X belongs to $+$	CHARACTERISTICS that distinguish X

If you use a verb (other than an infinitive) in Component C, you need to start C with a clause marker: *(prep.)* + *which, that,* or *who(m)*.

> EXAMPLES: *Laughter is a psychological expression **that** signals mastery over fear.*

Now, write formal definitions for the phenomena below with the information given. Because the characteristics below are expressed with verbs, you need to use *(prep.)* + *which, that,* or *who(m)*. Follow this general rule in choosing a clause marker for Component C:

CLAUSE MARKERS		EXAMPLES	
B (things or places)	+ (prep.) + *which*	. . . a room	*in which* people sleep
B (things, people, or places)	+ *that*	. . . a vehicle	*that* can transport . . .
B (people)	+ *who*	. . . a person	*who* teaches . . .
B (people)	+ (prep.) + *whom*	. . . a leader	*in whom* people trust

In the exercise on page 71, be sure that the verbs agree with their subjects.

1. Color blindness . . . eye disorder . . . cause a person to confuse reds with greens.

   What is *color blindness*? _____

   _____

2. Earthquakes . . . movements of the earth . . . result from internal pressure.

   What are *earthquakes*? _____

   _____

3. Rickets . . . bone disease . . . result from a lack of Vitamin D.

   What is *rickets*? _____

   _____

4. Satisfaction . . . psychological response . . . come from achieving a goal.

   What is *satisfaction*? _____

   _____

5. Friendship . . . emotional bond between two people . . . like and respect each other.

   What is *friendship*? _____

   _____

6. A microscope . . . optical instrument . . . use lenses to magnify images.

   What is a *microscope*? _____

   _____

7. A biologist . . . scientist . . . study living organisms.

   What is a *biologist*? _____

   _____

8. A conversation . . . spoken exchange between or among people . . . want to express their thoughts, opinions, and feelings.

   What is a *conversation*? _____

   _____

Exercise D: Writing Illustrations

Part I

In all English writing, and in expository writing in particular, there is constant movement between generalizations and specific details. The specific details are usually examples and illustrations of the generalizations.

EXAMPLE: Generalization *According to psychologists, laughter expresses our mastery over fear and worry.*

Illustration *Picture what happens when a parent takes a young child into a swimming pool. At first, the child may be frightened and even cry. However, once the child feels secure, he or she will laugh, splash, and enjoy the water.*

In the exercise below, match the illustrations (A–E) to the generalizations (1–5). Copy the appropriate illustration under its generalization.

Illustrations

A. For example, people speak more formally in a government office than they do at home.

B. There are only four pieces of furniture arranged on a beige rug.

C. Picture a student who laughs easily before a big exam. The student is saying, "See, this isn't bothering me. I am the master of this situation."

D. For instance, a woman may talk in a different way to her daughter, her mother, and her secretary.

E. If a person wants to analyze a problem, he/she will speak about "reasons" and "factors," but if he/she wants to complain about a problem, he/she may ask "why" questions and make negative statements.

Generalizations

1. The living room area of the Cooper house is simply furnished.

_____

_____

2. Spoken language changes according to the purpose of the conversation.

   _____

   _____

3. People laugh when they are afraid or nervous because they want to pretend to be in control.

   _____

   _____

4. The place of a conversation has an effect on spoken language.

   _____

   _____

5. The relationship of the people in a conversation affects spoken language.

   _____

   _____

Part II

Complete each short text below with your own illustration. If the generalization does not seem true to you, change it slightly. Use one or more of the following to begin your illustration:

> for example   picture what happens when . . .
> for instance   if . . .
> to illustrate

> EXAMPLE: *My ideal husband would be kind and thoughtful.*
> For example, if I were sick, he would put me to bed, prepare some chicken soup for me, and call the doctor if necessary.

1. There are times in the American culture when it is important to call people by their last names.

    _____

    _____

    _____

2. Anger is often expressed in a very direct way.

    _____

    _____

    _____

3. Convenience is one definite advantage of owning a car.

    _____

    _____

    _____

4. Honesty is one of the most important human qualities.

    _____

    _____

    _____

5. English is an important international language.

    _____

    _____

    _____

Exercise E: Introducing a Topic

The introduction to a composition, especially an expository one, narrows from a few general statements that present the central topic to a statement or two that pinpoint the controlling idea of the composition. Try to visualize the introduction as a narrowing of the writer's focus and the point from which the body flows:

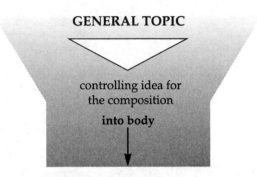

In the exercise below, read introductory paragraphs to three different compositions. (Only the introductions are given here.) Then state the general topic and the controlling idea of each one.

EXAMPLE: *Some people giggle quietly. Others let loose with hearty laughter.*
However we laugh, laughter is a necessary ingredient of a happy,
healthy life. We can easily recognize laughter, but what exactly is it?

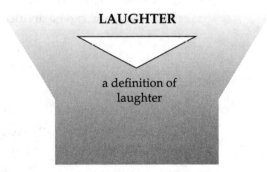

Introduction 1

Learning to understand spoken English is difficult. What makes it difficult is that the same person speaks differently in different situations. In their analyses, sociolinguists cite three major factors that affect spoken English.

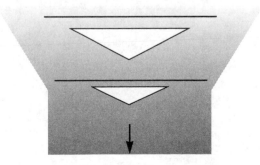

Introduction 2

Each society has its own way of treating the elderly. In many parts of the world, old people live with their children and grandchildren who care for them. This is the custom in Asia and in many Latin American countries. In the United States, however, old people often live alone or in nursing homes. Sometimes, the old people themselves insist upon this arrangement. More often, however, it is the attitude of the younger people in the family that determines the arrangement.

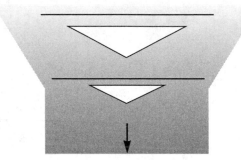

Introduction 3

Early inhabitants of the earth were not controlled so much by time. They had no planes to catch or classes to attend. Their clocks were the rising and setting of the sun, the shape of the moon in the night sky, and the change of seasons. Then, as the inhabitants began to live in groups, time became more important. Simple devices for measuring separate periods of time were developed. Later, more complex instruments were invented. Overall, the development of instruments for measuring time can be divided into four stages.

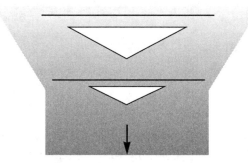

Preliminary Writing

You and your teacher can decide which of the following activities to do. Write in your journal or in a special notebook.

1. Make a list of concepts that might be interesting to define. Make another list of commonplace, everyday objects that would be interesting to define. Make a third list of jobs or professions that might be interesting to define; list them in terms of the person who does the job, e.g., a *nurse* or a *gardener*.

2. Look up the word "cancer" in your dictionary. Write out the definition. Who might define "cancer" this way? Write out a brief definition of "cancer" from the point of view of a cancer patient. Write out another brief definition from the point of view of a young child whose father is dying of cancer.

3. You read about laughter in Reading 4. Write briefly about a time you remember when you laughed long and hard about something. When was it? Where were you? What happened? What caused you to laugh? Describe your laughter.

4. Write briefly about something you have spent a lot of time trying to define. What is *true love*? What is *brotherhood*? What is a *good parent*? What is *happiness*? etc. What different definitions have you come up with? Why is it (whatever *it* is) difficult to define?

5. Choose five items from your lists (number 1 above). For each item, make a list of all the possible details that come to mind—physical characteristics, uses, examples, causes, effects, analogies, qualities, etc.

Instructions for Composition 4

Follow the instructions below as you write.

1. Choose a topic that you can define: a person, place, object, process, or concept. Concepts are probably the hardest to define. You might choose a topic that is unfamiliar to your reader. For example, you might define *photosynthesis* to someone who knows nothing about biochemistry. In this case, you would write to inform, or explain. On the other hand, you might choose a topic that is very familiar to the reader, but you might define it in a personal or creative way. (See the list of suggested topics in the following section.)

2. After you choose your topic, decide on a plan of development. You might define your topic several times and have each definition add to a fuller definition (as in Reading 4). This would be a good way to define a person, place, or concept. If you wanted to define an object, you might want to develop your essay with a physical description and a list of uses. If you wanted to define a process, you would need to explain briefly the process, step by step.

3. Jot down ideas and details as they come to mind. Look over your notes and circle whatever you want to build into your composition.

4. Write a draft of your composition. Then read through it several times, making changes as you go. You may need to prepare a clean draft after your changes.

5. Make sure that your clean draft has a title; check to be sure that you have left wide margins and that each paragraph is indented. Your teacher will give you instructions at this point.

Suggested Topics for Composition 4

Your teacher will ask you to write one or more compositions using definition as a means of development. Here are some suggested topics:

Composition A

Define something that you know about from personal experience. In order to be sure that your definition is comprehensive, write a list of questions about the topic before you begin. In this way you will be sure to leave nothing out. (You should assume that the reader knows nothing about the topic, or has never thought about it in the way that you have chosen to write about it.) Here are some possibilities:

1. Define your favorite sport:

   What is it? What physical activity is involved? How many people participate at one time? Why is it played? When is it played? Where is it played? Who plays it? How is it played? What special equipment is required?

2. Define a person who does a particular job; for example, define a *waiter*, a *bus driver*, a *soldier*, a *student*, a *baby-sitter*, a *store clerk*, etc. Include details about the following:

   What does the person do? What are the responsibilities of the job? What are the duties of the job? What training or experience does the person need? Who hires the person? Where does the person do this job? How much is the person paid? What might this job lead to? What social status does this person have?

Composition B

Define something that permits you to use your special cultural perspective. In other words, let the reader view something through the eyes of someone (you!) from a different culture. You might want to add humor (or sadness) to your definition. Here are some possibilities; you ask the detailed questions.

1. What is a *hamburger*?

2. What are *jeans*?

3. What is *fast food*?

4. What is a *day-care center*?

5. What is a *nursing home*?

Composition C

Define something about which you have special knowledge. You are the authority on this subject and you are defining it for the general public. (You might need to do some research to get details.) Here are some possibilities:

1. Define *dyslexia*. What is it? What are its causes? What are its effects? Who has it? etc. (Check a medical encyclopedia for information. Also check the *Readers' Guide* in the library for periodicals.)

2. Define a *stranger*. What is a stranger? Who defines a person as a stranger? What are the feelings of a stranger? What are the hazards of being a stranger? What are the benefits of being a stranger? What are the conditions for remaining a stranger? What are the conditions for *not* remaining a stranger? (Check sociology source books, or use your own experience as a resource; you might also include the experience of friends to illustrate your points.)

UNIT 5

Posing Hypothetical
Situations

Composition Focus:	*Hypothetical narration*
Organizational Focus:	*Chronological order*
Grammatical Focus:	*Conditionals*

Study the photo and illustrations. Describe what you see in each one.

- Is a wood stove the only way to heat?
- Why can't rooms in a skyscraper be heated this way?
- What dishes (meals) can be cooked on a wood stove?
- How long would it take you to travel to school or work by bicycle? On foot? By horse?
- Overall, what other differences can you imagine if you lived without electricity or petroleum?

WHAT IF...

(1)   In industrialized countries, people are highly dependent on petroleum fuel. Economists, conservationists, and political leaders constantly warn us about this dependence. They encourage us to drive less, turn down our heat, and turn off lights. Yet it is hard for people to change their ways. We take our modern conveniences so much for granted; it would be difficult to imagine ourselves returning to an earlier way of life.

(2)   Without gas or electricity, in particular, a person's daily routine would be considerably different. Each winter morning, it would be necessary to build a fire in the fireplace or wood stove; this would warm the house. In the summer, it would be necessary to bring the bedding in from the porch, or wherever people slept to keep cool. There would, of course, be no fans or air conditioners. Breakfast would be cooked over a fire. Water for shaving and for washing would have to be heated over a fire. All of this would take a lot of time.

(3)   A person would travel to school or work by bicycle, by horse, or on foot. It would be convenient to live near the school or place of work; there would certainly be no long-distance commuters! At school or at the office, there would be no copy machines, no electric typewriters, and no coffee-makers. On dark days, lamps that burn animal oil would provide light. Lunches would be brought from home.

(4)   Preparing supper would take up a lot of time in the late afternoon or early evening. Dairy products and meat would have to be bought daily. Schoolwork would be done by the light of an oil lamp. Bathwater would have to be heated over a fire and bedtime would come early.

(5)   On the whole, life would be simpler because people would try to do less. It would be impossible to go to five different places in one day! Life would be harder, too. People would suffer more from the heat and cold. Food preparation would take more work. All the modern conveniences that make life easier would be missing. We would return to the way of life of our great-grandparents. We would also experience the way of life that many people in the world—in non-industrialized countries—experience every day.

Author's note: When my mother (who is still alive) was a girl, she rode a horse to school. When my sister and I started school, we walked two miles (3.2 km.) in each direction. The changes I write about in Reading 5 are not ancient ones; many of them have taken place in the lives of people still living! There are still, of course, rural families around the world who live without electricity or running water.

Complete the following lists with information from Reading 5.

A. Morning routine without gas or electricity

    1.

    2.

    3.

    4.

B. Work or school routine without gas or electricity

    1.

    2.

C. Evening routine without gas or electricity

    1.

    2.

    3.

Let your teacher guide you through the following notes and questions.

1. When you think and write about past, present, and future possibilities, you are speculating or *hypothesizing*:

   What would have happened if . . . ?
   What would happen if . . . ?
   What will happen if . . . ?

   English grammar has special forms for this. Hypothesizing can be fun, if you ask a question such as this: *What would you do if someone gave you a million dollars?* Hypothesizing can also be serious, if you ask a question such as this: *What would happen to Los Angeles if its source of water ran dry?*

   In Reading 5, is the subject serious, lighthearted, or somewhere in between?

2. In an unreal hypothesis, there are two basic components: an unreal, untrue condition and an unreal, untrue consequence.

   Look at the following examples:

UNREAL:		
	past time consequence	**past time condition**
	I would have seen you yesterday	*if you had come .* (You didn't come.)
SAME GRAMMAR!	**present time consequence**	**present time condition**
	I would study now	*if I could could find my book.* (I can't find it.)
	future time consequence	**future time condition**
	I would go to Europe tomorrow	*if someone gave me the money.* (Nobody is going to give me the money.)
POSSIBLY REAL:		
	future time consequence	**future time condition**
	I will go to the language lab	*if I have time.* (Maybe I will have time.)

A *past* unreal condition can, however, produce a *present* unreal consequence. Look at the following example:

UNREAL:

present time consequence	**past time condition**
I would still be in Chicago (now)	*if my uncle hadn't invited me to New Orleans last summer.* (He invited me.)

Look at Reading 5. What is the condition? What are the consequences? How many consequences are there? Are the conditions and consequences in the same time frame?

3. Writers usually talk about a real situation before they hypothesize about unreal possibilities. You should do that too.

In the first paragraph of Reading 5, where does the writer shift from real to unreal? What phrase begins the hypothesis?

4. A narrative can be hypothetical, as in Reading 5. What purpose do you think the narrative serves? It should serve a purpose; it should help to clarify something. Look at the body of Reading 5. How is the narrative organized? How is it divided?

5. The conclusion to a hypothetical narrative usually shifts the reader back to reality. At which point does this happen in Reading 5?

Before going on to the exercises, briefly discuss the changes that make the key differences for you between an "earlier way of life" and your present way of life. What are the differences between your way of life and that of your parents? Your grandparents?

Exercise A: Stating Condition and Consequence

Part I

Complete each sentence below by stating a *consequence*. The first half of the sentence states a present condition that is unreal and untrue. For that reason, the condition requires past tense grammar, even though the time is present. When you write a consequence of the condition, use *would, could,* or *might.* Then the grammar of the two halves will agree.

> EXAMPLE: *If there were no automobiles,* <u>people would walk more</u> .

1. If there were no air conditioners, _____

   _____

2. If there were no refrigerators, _____

   _____

3. If there were no hot-water heaters, _____

   _____

4. If there were no electric lights, _____

   _____

5. If there were no automatic washing machines, _____

   _____

Part II

Complete each sentence below by writing a present *condition.* To show that your condition is unreal and untrue, use the *past tense.*

> EXAMPLE: *It would take longer for people to get to work if they* <u>had to walk.</u>

1. Students would do their homework by candlelight or oil lamp if _____

   _____

2. People would suffer from the heat if _____

_____

3. People would bathe less often if _____

_____

4. Students would walk or ride bicycles to school if _____

_____

5. People would have to buy their meat and dairy products fresh daily if _____

_____

_____

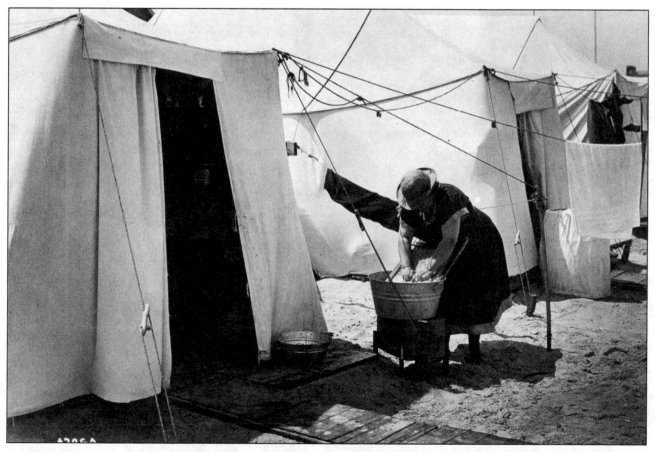

▲ If there were no automatic washing machines, people would have to wash their clothes by hand.

Exercise B: Shortening Sentences

Reduce the first half of each sentence (the *if* clause) to a prepositional phrase; change *if there were no* to *without*. Here, the meaning is the same. Rewrite the whole sentence.

> EXAMPLE: *If there were no gas or electricity, life would be different.*
>
> <u>Without gas or electricity, life would be different.</u>

1. If there were no air conditioning, people would suffer from the heat.

   _____

2. If there were no gas or electric stoves, people could cook on wood stoves.

   _____

3. If there were no hot water heaters, people could heat their water over a fire.

   _____

4. If there were no clocks, people might tell time by looking at the sun.

   _____

5. If there were no automatic washing machines, people would have to wash their clothes by hand or with manually-operated machines.

   _____

Exercise C: Using the Passive

Use ideas from Reading 5 to state the hypothetical consequences of having no gas or electricity. Use the passive voice and the following passive construction:

> would
> could   +   be   +   past participle
> might

EXAMPLE: *Without gas or electricity, a fire* <u>would (have to) be built in the fireplace or wood stove each morning.</u>

Note: You might want to use *have to + be* when you use *would* or *might*.

1. Without gas or electricity, the house _____

   _____

2. Without gas or electricity, breakfast _____

   _____each morning.

3. Without gas or electricity, water for shaving, bathing, and washing dishes

   _____

4. Without gas or electricity, bicycles or horses _____

   _____

5. Without gas or electricity, lunches _____

   _____

6. Without gas or electricity, a lot of time _____

   _____

   _____in the late afternoon or early evening.

7. Without gas or electricity, meat and dairy products _____

    _____

8. Without gas or electricity, schoolwork _____

    _____

▲ Without running water, water for shaving, bathing, and washing dishes could be drawn from a well.

Exercise D: Using the Filler *It* in Conditionals

Answer each set of questions below with a single sentence. Answer the questions in a general way with your own ideas. Since the questions are hypothetical, your answer will also be hypothetical. Use the following construction:

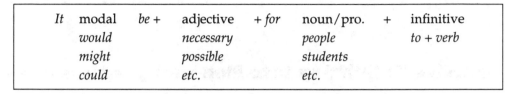

It	modal	*be +*	adjective	*+ for*	noun/pro.	*+*	infinitive
	would		*necessary*		*people*		*to + verb*
	might		*possible*		*students*		
	could		*etc.*		*etc.*		

EXAMPLE: *What if there were no system of currency? How would people buy goods?*

It would be possible for them to barter.

1. What if there were no instruments for telling time? How would people regulate their activities?

_____

2. What if there were no indoor plumbing? How would people bathe?

_____

3. What if there were no glass containers? How would people drink liquids and store their goods?

_____

4. What if there were no public transportation? How would people get from one place to another?

_____

5. What if there were no writing paper? How would students do their school work?

_____

6. What if there were no houses? How would people live?

_____

7. What if there were no schools? How would people learn?

_____

8. What if there were no bridges? How would people cross streams and rivers?

_____

Exercise E: Shifting into Nonreality

Hypothetical topics are fascinating. _What would happen if . . . ?_ It is interesting to speculate and imagine. When you write hypothetically, first establish reality. Tell the reader what is real. Then, you can shift to nonreality.

In the following paragraphs, locate where the writer shifts from reality to non-reality. Below each paragraph, a) write the phrase that creates the shift and b) predict what would follow if the composition continued.

> EXAMPLE: I_n industrialized countries, people are highly dependent on gas and electricity. Economists and political leaders constantly warn us about this dependence. They encourage us to conserve energy by driving less, turning down heaters, and turning off lights. We have taken modern conveniences so much for granted that it would be hard to imagine daily life without gas or electricity at all._
>
> a)   Phrase signaling shift to nonreality:
>   _. . . it would be hard to imagine . . ._
>
> b)   Predicted development of following paragraphs:
>   _a hypothetical day without gas or electricity . . ._

Paragraph 1

   Early inhabitants of the earth were not so controlled by time. They had no planes to catch or time clocks to punch. Their clocks were the sun, the moon, and the change of seasons. Modern life is so regulated by measured time that it would be difficult to imagine daily life in a technological society without any clocks at all.

a) Phrase signaling shift to nonreality: _____

_____

b) Predicted development of following paragraphs: _____

_____

Paragraph 2

Since the days of Julius Caesar, many human societies have lived according to a calendar divided into 12 months. Most species of animals, however, live by a more basic calendar. Their calendar depends on the Earth's position and movements in the solar system. Suppose that we lived by the solar calendar. Our activities would be seasonal, not daily, weekly, or monthly.

a) Phrase signaling shift to nonreality:_____

_____

b) Predicted development of following paragraphs: _____

_____

Paragraph 3

Migrations are a survival mechanism developed by people and animals to expand their food supply and to cope with seasonal changes in climate. Each year, monarch butterflies, for example, fly thousands of miles from southern Canada and the northern United States to California and Mexico. Each spring, elephant seals swim from the coast of California to the Aleutian Islands. Although a few traditional human societies still follow migratory cycles, modern societies have developed other means of coping with changes in climate and food supply. Try to picture the effects on our lives if we had to migrate seasonally in search of food and sunshine.

a) Phrase signaling shift to nonreality:_____

_____

b) Predicted development of following paragraphs: _____

_____

Preliminary Writing

You and your teacher can decide which of the following activities to do. Write in your journal or in a special notebook.

1. Make a list of the appliances and machines around you without which your daily life would change. Make a second and shorter list of those that you would hate to give up the most.

2. Write briefly about how your life would be different in your culture if you were of the opposite sex. What could you do that you can't do now? What couldn't you do that you can do now?

3. Write briefly about how you would change your present way of life if you could. What would you need to change? How would your life change?

4. If you could be someone else for a day (a famous actor, the Queen of England, Abraham Lincoln, etc.), who would you be? Write about your day.

5. If you were an animal, what animal would you be? An elephant? A pigeon? A whale? etc. Why would you be this particular animal? What would you do? Where would you live? What would you like about your life? What would the problems be?

▲ How would your daily life change if there were no cars?

Instructions for Composition 5

Follow the instructions below as you write.

1. Choose a present or future unreal situation with possible effects on your daily life or the lives of others. You might choose a topic that is humorous, or you might choose one that is very serious. For example, *how would your daily life be different if you were a parent of twenty children*? (Surely you could find some humor in that!) On the other hand, a topic such as this would be serious and sad: *What would your daily life be like if you never had enough food to eat*? (Check the suggested topics on the next page.)

2. As you choose your topic, think about the points you want to make with your narrative. With the topics above as examples, you might want to humorously emphasize the perils and joys of parenthood, or you might want to focus on the awful effects of hunger.

3. Then decide on your plan of development. You should begin with reality and then narrow down to the unreal condition for the unreal consequences you are going to relate. Decide on how to develop the consequences chronologically within the boundaries of one day or some other period of time. Make notes as you think about this; jot down what comes to mind.

4. Write a draft of your composition. Then read through it several times, making changes as you go. More ideas will come to mind as you work. You may need to prepare a clean draft after your changes.

5. Make sure that your clean draft has a title; check margins and paragraph indentation. Your teacher will give you instructions at this point.

Suggested Topics for Composition 5

Your teacher will ask you to write one or more hypothetical narratives. Here are some suggestions.

Composition A

Hypothesize about what your life would be like if you were living under different circumstances. If it is appropriate, be humorous. Here are some ideas:

1. How would your daily life be different if you were married? If you are married, how would your life be different if you were single?

2. How would your daily life be different if you had children? If you have a small family, you might hypothesize about a larger family. How would your daily life be different if you had *many* children?

3. What would your typical day be like now if you were still in your native country?

4. How would your life be different if you lived under a different political system? Identify and describe the system. Explain and illustrate specific differences.

5. If a flying saucer descended tonight and you went aboard, what would your experience be like? Describe your ride, the ship, and your traveling companions.

Composition B

Hypothesize about what twentieth-century life would be like if many of the things around us disappeared. Let your ideas help the reader develop a sharper perspective on modern life. Be positive or negative. Give details.

1. How would our daily lives be changed if there were no system of currency (no coins, no bills)? Take the reader through a typical day: buying morning coffee, taking the bus to work, buying lunch, getting home, doing the grocery shopping. Devise a substitute for money.

2. How would a person's daily routine change if there were no paper products? Take the reader through a typical day. How would a person compensate? What would a person write on? What would happen to a "fast food" lunch?

3. How would daily life be affected if there were no automobiles, buses, trains, or airplanes? What would a typical day look like? How would people travel about? How would the movements of people, ideas, goods, etc., be affected?

4. How would daily life change if nobody were literate? Describe a typical day without reading anything (cereal boxes, newspapers, traffic signs, restroom doors, street addresses, clocks, billboards, books, etc.)! What system of giving information could replace writing?

Composition C

Hypothesize about something in a particular professional field. Do research, if necessary, in order to become more knowledgeable on the subject. Here are some possibilities:

1. You think that there are serious problems with the system of education in this country or in your native country. Describe a typical school day as it would be under your improved system. (You might check a basic education textbook for educational vocabulary, but you probably know details already.)

2. You are concerned about the effects of inflation. Discuss the changes in daily life that would result from a continued rise in the rate of inflation. How would life be affected if the rate were double what it is now? Talk about the effects on the economy of a particular country. Include details. (Check the *Readers' Guide* in the library for the latest economic publications.)

3. You are interested in how people in a technological society could live more simply and peacefully. Describe the typical day of a person who lives closer to nature in a cabin in the woods. What would that person do? What would that person see? How would that person live?

Unit 6

Seeing *Differences* and *Similarities*

C. 1960s–1970s: Detroit's suburbs bloom.

Composition Focus: Comparison and contrast

Organizational Focus: Contrastive balance

Grammatical Focus: Comparative sentences

AUTO SALES

	1970	1973	1976	1979	1982	
	84.8%	84.7%	85.2%	78.1%	72.2%	Domestic
	3.7%	6.5%	9.3%	16.6%	22.6%	Japanese
	8.9%	6.9%	3.7%	3.3%	3.1%	German
	2.6%	1.9%	1.8%	2.0%	2.1%	Other
Total Sales (in millions)	8.40	11.42	10.11	10.67	7.98	

Study the photos and chart.

- What do you see in A and B? What is the subject?
- What trend is shown in B?
- What do you suppose is the connection between B and D?
- What is the difference between C and D?
- Look at the title of Reading 6: What do you think it means?

B. 1970s: Detroit's auto industry feels the effects of foreign competition.

A. 1940s–1960s: Detroit's automobile industry is booming.

D. 1970s, 1980s: Detroit's central city withers.

TWO CITIES IN ONE

(1) After World War II, the American automobile industry boomed. Thousands of men and women looking for work flocked to Detroit, where General Motors, Ford, and other major American automakers had located their plants. In Detroit, even semi-skilled workers could expect to get jobs and earn good money. Detroit became known as Motor City, U.S.A.—the City on the Go.

(2) Today, Detroit is called Murder Capital, U.S.A. What happened to America's seventh-largest city? How could the City on the Go, with its booming economy, decline into poverty and violence? Detroit is now two cities. One is predominantly white and prosperous, with its residents living in the suburbs; the other is predominantly black and poor, with its residents living in the central area. White residents began leaving the central city in the mid-1950s, when their higher-paying jobs allowed them to move "up" by moving "out" to new homes in the suburbs. The exodus became a mass evacuation after July 1967. At that time, riots in the central city left 43 dead and thousands of buildings burned. Everybody who could afford to leave did.

(3) The decline accelerated in the 1970s as the American auto industry felt the effects of foreign competition. Jobs in the auto plants dried up and workers were laid off. Store owners relocated their businesses as their clientele changed. As store owners moved away, the city's tax base shrank. As a result, city services, such as police protection and garbage collection, declined. Central Detroit became home to people who were poor and had no place else to go. Now, with over a third of its residents gone, the population of central Detroit is barely a million; and the city that was once multiracial is now 75 percent black.

(4)   What can be done? The residents of central Detroit are trying to figure that out. Led by the city's first and current African-American mayor, Coleman Young, over 800 community groups have organized themselves to fight drugs, street crime, teenage pregnancy, and joblessness. City leaders have recently persuaded the Chrysler Corporation to locate its new state-of-the-art auto plant in Detroit, opening up new jobs for local residents. The problems, however, are daunting, and the road to economic and social recovery is long.

Author's note: To read about the failures and successes of other large cities in the United States, check the following issues of *National Geographic*:
Pittsburgh—Vol. 180, No. 6 (1991): 125–145;
Atlanta—Vol. 174, No. 1 (1988): 3–29;
Indianapolis—Vol. 172, No. 2 (1987): 230–259;
Washington, D.C.—Vol. 163, No. 1 (1983): 84–125.

TOLL OF 1967 DETROIT RIOTS— SECOND WORST IN U.S. HISTORY

KILLED—At least 43, including one policeman and one fireman.

INJURED—About 2,000.

FIRES REPORTED—About 1,400.

STORES LOOTED—About 1,700.

PROPERTY DAMAGE—Upwards of 250 million dollars.

TOTAL COST—1 billion dollars.

▲ A homeless man in downtown Detroit

Taking Notes

Compare Detroit of the 1940s–1960s to Detroit of today by completing the information below. Check back to Reading 6 for your wording.

DETROIT: Two Cities in One

1940s–1960s: "Motor City"

1. booming economy

2. many jobs in auto industry

3. major retailers located in city

4. large tax base

5. good municipal services

6. population: white and prosperous

7. population: 1.5 million

1990s: "_____"

1. _____

2. _____

3. _____

4. _____

5. _____

6. _____

7. _____

Notes and Questions on Reading 6

Let your teacher guide you through the following notes and questions.

1. When writers compare, they look at similarities. When they contrast, they look at differences. Writers often compare and contrast in the same composition. Sometimes, they give equal space to the differences and the similarities; other times, the focus is on one or the other. In Reading 6, what is the overall focus—differences or similarities?

2. When you start thinking about a topic that you want to compare and/or contrast, you have to decide which aspect(s) of that topic you want to examine. Take, for example, the topic *my two brothers*. Let's say that you want to write about their personalities. You might think that their personalities are similar in some ways, but different in others. Now you have a controlling idea!

   You might further subdivide the controlling idea into aspects of their personalities, such as personal qualities and interests. Then you take each aspect and go back and forth from one brother to the other. For example, when you are writing about their interests, you might say that *John is more interested in sports than Paul, but they both like classical music.*

   In Reading 6, what are the subdivisions?

3. English has a lot of special vocabulary for comparison and contrast. Here are some special words and phrases for *similarities*:

VOCABULARY	EXAMPLES
alike	I have two bothers who look exactly *alike*, but they're not twins.
as _____ as	My younger sister is *as* tall *as* I am.
both	My sister and I *both* love ice cream.
in the same way	People say that my father and I smile *in* exactly *the same way*.
(just) like	My younger brother looks *just like* me.
likewise	My mother laughs when she's nervous; my brother does *likewise*.
resemble	Some people say that I *resemble* my maternal grandmother.
similar _____ to	The house we live in now is *similar* in design *to* our old house.
similarly	My father was raised to treat everyone courteously and respectfully. He expects his children to behave *similarly*.

the same _____ as	My hair is *the same* color *as* my mother's.
similarity	My mother thinks that I bear a striking *similarity* to my grandmother.

You might need some of the following when you are discussing *differences*:

although	*Although* my older brother likes baseball, my younger brother hates it!
differ from	How does your family *differ from* mine?
different from	Even twins are often *different from* each other in personality.
even so	My brother had a hard time passing his geometry course. *Even so*, he persisted and finally got through.
even though	*Even though* geometry was difficult for my brother, he didn't give up.
however	My father loves to watch football games on television; *however*, my mother can't stand them.
in contrast to	*In contrast to* my mother, my father is tall and thin.
nevertheless	My mother and father have very different personalities. *Nevertheless*, they get along well.
on the contrary	Most members of my family thought that my younger brother would grow up to be talkative and outgoing. *On the contrary*, he is quiet and shy.
otherwise	People expected him to run away from a fight. He did *otherwise*.
unalike	Two people could not be more *unalike* than my two sisters.
yet	My grandmother is old and frail, *yet* she cooks her own meals and takes care of herself.

Many of these words and phrases can occur in more than one position in a sentence. FOR EXAMPLE: *My father was raised to treat everyone courteously and respectfully. He expects his children to behave similarly.*

My father was raised to treat everyone courteously and respectfully. Similarly, he raised us to be polite and respectful.

Ask your teacher about alternative ways to use the words and phrases on the list. You will need this vocabulary, especially if you compare/contrast two different subjects in the same time frame. (Since Reading 6 is about a single subject in different time frames, less contrastive vocabulary is needed.)

4. There is one last point to consider here. As a writer, your tone and attitude toward your subject are important elements in your composition. This point applies to all of your writing, not just comparison and contrast, and Reading 6 illustrates it well. Read the following example:

> *When I was a child, my grandfather was ten feet tall. As I grew older and taller, he amazingly grew older and shorter. By the time I was in high school, we were about the same height. By then, I saw him in a different light. He was no longer a superhuman figure, but I loved him just as much.*

We can say that the writer of these few sentences is an adult fondly remembering the past. The tone is warm and lighthearted, almost joking. The grandfather was never really ten feet tall, was he?

Look at the writer's relationship to Reading 6. Does the writer end on a pessimistic or optimistic note?

Before going on to the exercises, discuss with your classmates your own experience with urban change. Has the city or the town where you live changed during your time there? What about your hometown?

▲ Describe these twins, using the vocabulary you have learned for describing similarities.

Exercise A: Supplying Cohesion

Complete the sentences below with words or phrases from the following list:

> *however*—to show contrast
> *whether or not*—to state an optional condition
> *yet*—to show contrast
> *since*—to state cause
> *as*—to show corresponding time
> *as a result*—to state an effect
> *in fact*—to give more actual details
> *otherwise*—to show that something is opposite

> EXAMPLE: *Detroit was once a prosperous city. Today,* __however__ *, it is poor and violent.*

After checking your answers, write your own pairs of phrases or sentences using the words from the list. Verify the grammar and punctuation with your teacher and classmates.

═══════════════════════════════════════

1. _____ the city's tax base has shrunk, police protection and garbage collection have declined. Without a broad tax base, there is no money to pay for city services. (Note: The shrinking tax base is the cause of declining services.)

2. Many church groups in Detroit's central city are determined to rebuild their community _____ the federal government gives them financial help. They say that they'll do it alone if they have to.

3. The leaders of Detroit must convince business and industry to return to their city; _____ , they will not be able to expand the city's tax base.

4. The suburbs ringing Detroit are predominantly white. _____ , they are identified in one study as the most segregated in America.

5. The city's tax base shrank. _____ , city services, such as police and fire protection, have declined.

6. Detroit is not the only large city in the U.S. to fall on hard times. Its problems, _____ , are among the worst because its economy is based primarily on a single industry.

7. Detroit's decline accelerated in the 1970s _____ the American auto industry felt the effects of foreign competition.

8. Some think that it is too late to save Detroit, _____ over 800 community groups are determined to try.

Exercise B: Practicing Verb Forms

Complete the sentences below with the appropriate forms of the verbs in parentheses. You will need the following tenses and voices, shown here with the sample verb *consider*:

TENSE	ACTIVE	PASSIVE
Simple present	consider(s)	am/is/are considered
Simple past	considered	was/were considered
Present perfect (simple)	has/have considered	has/have been considered

EXAMPLE: Parents (be) __are__ people just like everyone else. When I (be) __was__ younger, however, I (think) __thought__ that they (be) __were__ not.

1. In the late 1940s, Detroit (*call*) _____ Motor City, U.S.A.; today, it (*call*) _____ Murder Capital, U.S.A.

2. In the U.S.A., education (*consider*) _____ an individual's right; in Tunisia, however, it (*consider*) _____ _____ a privilege.

3. In the 1970s, jobs in the auto plants in Detroit (*dry up*) _____ _____ and auto workers (*lay off*) _____ _____ .

4. Some say that war (*be*) _____ a biological necessity. In contrast, I say that war (*be*) _____ just a bad invention.

5. Recently, Detroit city leaders (*persuade*) _____ the Chrysler Corporation to locate its new plant there.

6. Recently the Chrysler Corporation (*persuade*) _____ _____ to build its new, state-of-the-art plant in Detroit.

7. A few years ago, smoking (*consider*) _____ an ordinary, normal activity. Nowadays, smoking (*consider*) _____ _____ an unacceptable activity by many and is actually illegal in public buildings in many states.

8. In the 1970s, Detroit's tax base (*shrink*) _____ when store owners (*relocate*) _____ their businesses to more prosperous areas.

Exercise C: Introducing Comparative Ideas

Part I

Each group of sentences below could be part of an introductory paragraph to a comparative composition. Study each group. Then on the lines below, note the general topic (in one word) and the controlling idea (in a phrase). Also, note the particular point of contrast that the following paragraphs (not here) would develop, as determined by the controlling idea.

> EXAMPLE: *Teachers are human beings like everyone else. When I was a child, however, I thought that they were gods—infallible and omnipotent.*
>
> **General topic:**   <u>teachers</u>
> **Controlling idea:**   <u>the writer's changing attitude</u>
> <u>toward teachers</u>
> **Point of contrast:**   <u>attitude of a child (then) vs.</u>
> <u>attitude of an adult (now)</u>

---

1. In Tunisia, education is considered a privilege. In the United States, however, it is considered an individual's right.

   General topic: _____

   Controlling idea: _____

   Point of contrast: _____

2. Marriage used to be considered a permanent institution. However, many now regard it as a temporary state.

   General topic: _____

   Controlling idea: _____

   Point of contrast: _____

3. Parents are people. They make mistakes like everyone else. As a child, however, I thought that my parents were perfect. They knew everything.

   General topic: _____

   Controlling idea: _____

   Point of contrast: _____

4. There are those who say that war is a biological necessity. It expresses man's aggressive nature. In contrast, I think that war is just a bad invention.

   General topic: _____

   Controlling idea: _____

   Point of contrast: _____

Part II

Choose two of the pairs of contrastive ideas below and experiment with sentences that would set up each of your contrasts. Write 2–4 sentences for each pair.

EXAMPLE: *Contrast your attitudes toward your siblings (brothers and sisters) now to your attitudes toward them when you were a child.*

My two sisters are now my closest friends. When I was a child, however, I thought they were nothing but trouble!

1. Contrast your views of men or women now to your views of boys or girls when you were a child.

2. Contrast the importance of religion in your culture to what you perceive to be the importance of religion in another culture.

3. Contrast the attitudes of parents or society toward dating in your culture to the parental or social attitudes toward dating that you perceive in the United States.

4. Contrast your views toward your parents now to your views toward your parents when you were a child.

Exercise D: Creating Parallel Constructions

Similar ideas are often expressed in similar constructions. This relationship of ideas is called a *parallelism*.

EXAMPLES: *People come in all sizes, shapes, and colors.*
(Parallel vocabulary: characteristics)
(Parallel grammar: plural nouns)

One part of Detroit is predominantly white and prosperous. The other is predominantly black and poor.
(Parallel vocabulary: almost identical words)
(Parallel grammar: independent clauses)

Now, write sentences that are parallel to those below. The questions in parentheses and your own knowledge will guide you in writing your sentences.

EXAMPLE: *Women in this country used to comprise a small part of the labor force.*
(What about *now?*)
Now, women comprise a large part of the labor force.

1. People in the United States used to consider education a privilege. (What about now?)

2. Some people say that war is a biological necessity. (What about others?)

3. Marriage used to be considered permanent. (What about now?)

4. Divorce used to be considered shameful. (What about now?)

5. People in the United States used to consider a car a luxury. (What about now?)

6. In the United States the life expectancy of women used to be shorter than the life expectancy of men. (What about now?)

Exercise E: Writing Sentences of Comparison

Use the following grammatical forms to write sentences of comparison:

more ADJ./ADV. *than*   *less* ADJ./ADV. *than*
ADJ./ADV. *-er than*   *not as* ADJ./ADV. *as*

The directions below will tell you what to include in each sentence.

EXAMPLE: *Compare the tax base of the city of Detroit in the early 1950s and now.*

In the 1950s, the tax base of Detroit was larger than it is now.

1. Compare people's attitude toward religion in your culture a generation ago and now.

2. Compare social attitudes toward women working a generation ago and now.

3. Compare the volume and frequency of air travel a generation ago and now.

4. Compare the general public's knowledge about the hazards of smoking a generation ago and now.

5. Compare the level of literacy in your country a generation ago and now.

Preliminary Writing

You and your teacher can decide which of the following activities to do. Write in your journal or in a special notebook.

1. Make several lists of the characteristics that people in your culture tend to use to label people as "desirable" mates, as "good" parents, as "successful" professionals, or as "obedient" children.

2. Make a list of the changes in your hometown since you were a child there. Be specific and list details. Then organize the differences visually, like the notes following Reading 6 on page 102.

3. Briefly compare and contrast your notions of "masculine" and "feminine." What are the characteristics of each?

4. Briefly contrast your *ideal X* from your *real X*. Concentrate on the differences between, for example, two houses, spouses, cars, jobs, or ways of life.

5. Make two lists of characteristics of people in general. Make one list of the characteristics that you consider significant; make the other list of those that you consider insignificant.

Instructions for Composition 6

Follow the instructions below as you prepare to write your own composition.

1. Choose a topic that you can examine for its similarities and/or differences. It can be a topic that you examine over time. For example, *what were your ideas and feelings about school when you were a child and what are they now?* Or, you can examine a topic where time is unimportant. For example, *how is your present school similar to or different from your former school?* The topic may be abstract (for example, *your attitudes*) or concrete (for example, *two rooms*). In any case, you will need to give details to help the reader understand the similarities and/or differences. (Check the topics on the following page if you need ideas.)

2. Decide what point(s) you want to make with your comparison and contrast. For example, do you want to show that one room is warm and cozy and another is cold and sterile? Do you want to show how your attitudes have matured?

3. Make lists of the details that illustrate similarities and/or differences. Read over your lists; add and subtract details as you go. Check with a classmate to see if he or she can offer any ideas.

4. Write a draft of your composition. After you've finished your draft, read it over several times. Make changes as you read. Ask a classmate to read it and tell you if anything seems unclear or incomplete.

5. After you have made changes, write out a clean draft. Doublecheck the margins, spelling, and indentation of your paragraphs; also doublecheck punctuation and capital letters. Let your teacher know when your draft is ready.

Suggested Topics for Composition 6

Your teacher will ask you to write one or more comparison/contrast compositions. Here are some suggested topics:

Composition A

Compare and contrast something that you can see. Use a lot of spatial and physical description to organize and illustrate your composition. Here are some ideas:

1. Compare and contrast the town where you are living now to your hometown.

2. Compare and contrast your living conditions now to your living conditions when you were a child.

3. Compare and contrast two houses or apartments—perhaps the one you live in now to the one you lived in as a child.

4. Compare and contrast two institutions.

5. Compare and contrast two pieces of furniture.

6. Compare and contrast two appliances, pieces of machinery, or pieces of equipment.

Composition B

Compare and contrast your own personal changes in attitude through the perspective of time. How did you feel then, or what did you think then? How do you feel now, or what do you think now? Perhaps your attitudes have changed because you have grown older and wiser; perhaps your attitudes have changed because you are now living in a different culture. Maybe both are causes for change. Be specific; you need to discuss attitudes toward something in particular. Here are some ideas:

1. Compare and contrast your attitudes as a child toward your brothers and sisters (siblings) *to* your attitudes now. Give examples of how your former attitudes were reflected in everyday life. What do you do now that is different?

2. Compare and contrast your attitudes as a child toward your parents *to* your attitudes now. Illustrate. What has caused the change?

3. Compare and contrast your attitudes as a child toward religion *to* your attitudes now. Give examples. Show how any changes in attitude affect your everyday life.

Composition C

Write a comparison/contrast composition about one of the following topics. Do research, if necessary, in order to get details.

1. Contrast the elementary-school system in your home country to the elementary-school system in another country. Give details about the students, their ages, their courses, tuition, etc.

2. Contrast social attitudes toward dating and marriage in your home country to attitudes in another country. Give details. If you are not sure about attitudes in another culture, then you might contrast the attitudes of older people in your native culture toward dating and marriage to the attitudes of younger people of the same culture (if you think they are different). You might interview older and younger people to be sure.

3. Contrast the standard of living in your country to what it used to be (*if* it is changing). Is the country becoming richer or poorer? Specify how the changes affect people's lives: jobs, housing, food, education, goods, etc. How does it affect vital services: transportation, postal delivery, the telephone system, etc?

4. Contrast the political situation in your country to what it used to be (*if* it is changing). In which direction is it going? Who is/was in charge? What liberties do/did people have? How do the changes affect everyday life? What do you predict for the future?

Practice Composition Exam: B

It's time for another practice test. Pretend that it is a real test. (Your teacher might actually want it to be a *real* test.) You have _____ minutes to write a composition. You may (not) use a dictionary. Follow your teacher's special instructions.

Exam B1: Write an extended definition of one of the following:
 a. a wedding ring or a (white) flag
 b. a garbage collector or an actor
 c. a mental institution or a hospital
 d. a topic chosen by you or your teacher

Exam B2: Write a hypothetical narrative on one of the following:
 a. What if you had to change all of your future plans?
 b. What if you could spend your birthday any way you wanted?
 c. What if you could change any or all of the rules of your school, your office, or your culture?
 d. a topic chosen by you or your teacher

Exam B3: Write a comparison/contrast on one of the following:
 a. Compare a manually-operated machine, instrument, or device to one that is automatic (but serves the same purpose).
 b. Compare the way you are studying English now to the way you have studied it before.
 c. Compare a traditional way of doing something in your culture (example: asking someone for a date, applying for a job, etc.) to a more modern way of doing the same thing (in the same culture).
 d. a topic chosen by you or your teacher

Unit 7

Describing a *Process*

The eruption of
Mt. St. Helens ▼

Composition Focus: *Process description*

Organizational Focus: *Chronological order*

Grammatical Focus: *Passive voice*

Study diagrams A and B.

- What does A show?
- What is a "plate"?
- What *are* these plates? How do they fit together? How fast do they move?
- How does diagram B relate to diagram A?
- What has created the volcanos in northwestern U.S.A.?
- In general, how are volcanos created?

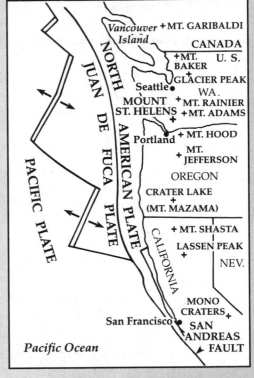

A. *Shifting Plates Cause Volcanic Eruptions*
The earth's surface is fragmented into plates. The plates pull apart, grind past each other, or slide beneath one another. This happens at a rate of about 8 inches, or 20 cm, each year.

B. *Enlargement of Northwestern U.S.A.*
The Juan de Fuca plate is sliding under the North American plate. As it slips and slides, it melts rock into pockets of magma far below the earth's surface.

WHEN MOUNTAINS ROAR

(1)   The eruption of a volcano is one of the earth's most spectacular displays of energy. Mount Pinatubo, a 4,765-foot volcano that began erupting in the Philippines in 1991, after 600 years of dormancy, released enough energy to send steam and ash more than ten kilometers high. Mount Tambora, a volcano in Indonesia that erupted in 1815, spewed over 80 cubic kilometers of ash and pumice into the atmosphere. As a result, the earth's temperature cooled, creating a year with no summer in 1816.

(2)   More than 300 active volcanos ring the Pacific Ocean alone, from Chile to Alaska, to Japan, and to New Zealand. Eleven major active volcanos form the Cascade Range in northwestern United States. When these land volcanos erupt, as Mount St. Helens in the Cascades did in 1980, it is the result of the plates of the earth's fragmented crust slipping and sliding. As they move, these immense plates create pressure far below the earth's surface.

(3)   Deep inside the earth, hot molten rock mixes with gas to create *magma*. Magma collects in chambers, around which the weight of the surrounding rock exerts enormous pressure. Gradually, under this intense pressure, the magma begins to rise. It rises through an opening, or *shaft*, in the weakened rock above. As the magma gets near the surface, gas is released, spewing magma, dust, and rock out of the crater at the top. The spewing of volcanic matter is the actual eruption.

(4)   Most volcanos erupt straight up through a central vent. Mt. Vesuvius, the volcano in Italy that destroyed the city of Pompeii in A.D. 79, erupted in this manner. However, some volcanos, such as Mt. St. Helens, erupt laterally through side vents. Lateral eruptions are particularly destructive because large areas of mountain are torn away with explosive force. (See the diagram that follows.) Either way, pressurized groundwater flashes into streams. Waves of superheated gas and melted rock, called *lava*, soon follow down the slopes, burying the surrounding valleys.

(5)   It takes millions of years for volcanos to form. It takes centuries more for them to build up to an eruption. Yet, in a matter of seconds, a volcano can blow apart in a hellish roar of destruction.

The Eruption of Mt. St. Helens

May 18, 1980:

1. BULGE
8:27:00 a.m.

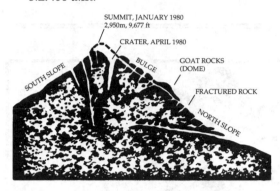

SUMMIT, JANUARY 1980
2,950m, 9,677 ft

CRATER, APRIL 1980

BULGE

GOAT ROCKS
(DOME)

FRACTURED ROCK

SOUTH SLOPE

NORTH SLOPE

3. BLAST
8:32:41 a.m.

LATERAL BLAST

2. LANDSLIDE
8:32:37 a.m.

DEBRIS
FLOW

4. SURGE
8:32:51 a.m.

Taking Notes

Reread "When Mountains Roar." Then, on the basis of information in the reading, fill in the missing terms following the explanations below the diagram. Finally, write the numbers on the appropriate lines of the diagram.

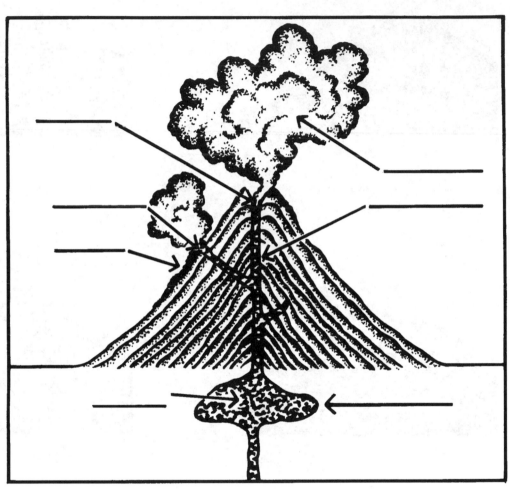

1. the mixture of hot molten rock mixed with gas:_____

2. the area in which rock and gas mixture collects:_____

3. the opening through which the mixture rises:_____

4. three different substances spewed out at the top:_____,

   _____, _____

5. the opening at the top:_____

6. an opening on the side:_____

7. the superheated mixture of gas and melted rock that flows down the

   sides:_____

Unit 7 ● Describing a Process

Notes and Questions on Reading 7

Let your teacher guide you through the following notes and questions.

1. A process is a connected series of actions, or steps, that leads to an end. You do X and Y in order to get to Z: (you) pour boiling water on a teabag and let it steep in order to have a cup of tea (a most complex procedure!!). That is a *how-to-do-it* process. It is written to instruct. The writer expects the reader to take some action.

   There is another kind of process as well, a *how-it-is-done* or *how-it-happens* process. It is written to inform, not to instruct. The writer expects no action from the reader. Certain topics can be developed either way: how to construct a bookcase, or how a bookcase is constructed. (You can see how each approach can require different grammar.) Other topics, usually natural, mechanical, and scientific processes, are described according to the second approach.

   > EXAMPLE: *How does a tadpole change into a frog? How does a carburetor work? What happens in photosynthesis?*

2. Most operational process descriptions follow a simple chronological (time) order. (*First, . . . Then, . . . Next, . . . Finally, . . .*) Steps usually occur one after the other. Sometimes, however, one or two steps may occur at the same time.

   Look back at Reading 7. Decide which steps in the volcanic process occur one after the other (*sequential* steps) and which occur at the same time (*simultaneous* steps).

   In Unit 2 (Notes and Questions), you will find a list of time words and phrases that can also be used in process description.

3. The *order* of the steps is very important to the description. If the steps are unclear, the description will be unclear. A writer also needs to add details about the process in order to make it clear. Pick out one step in the eruption of a volcano (Reading 7) and identify the supporting details that go with it.

4. As you can see in Reading 7, a lot of the information can be included at the beginning and at the end of a process description.

Look at the introduction to Reading 7. How does the writer try to get you interested in the topic? In other words, how does the writer try to make the topic more dramatic?

Look at the last two paragraphs. They are more than a summary of the process; new information is included. What is the relationship between the new information and the process?

Before going on to the exercises in Unit 7, tell your classmates if there are volcanos in your home country. If so, has one erupted in your lifetime or that of your parents or grandparents? Also, brainstorm about other natural processes. Make a list. Which ones are long-term, such as a volcano building up to an eruption, and which are short-term?

Exercise A: Practicing the Passive

Complete the sentences below with either *present* or *past passive* constructions. Each sentence below is in the present unless a time expression or the meaning of the sentence clearly marks it as past. Remember that the present (simple) and past (simple) passives look like this:

Simple present passive:	**Simple past passive:**

am
is   +   past participle
are

was
         +   past participle
were

EXAMPLE: *Power (release)* ___is released___ *at the top of a volcano.*

1. The power released by a volcano *(generate)* _____ far below the earth's surface.

2. Magma *(create)* _____ by hot molten rock mixing with gas.

3. Pressure *(exert)* _____ by the weight of the rock around the chamber of magma.

4. Gas *(release)* _____ as the magma gets near the surface.

5. The actual eruption of a volcano (*cause*) _____ by gas spewing volcanic matter out of the top of the volcano.

6. Some molten rock and dust (*release*) _____ through side vents.

7. When Mt. St. Helens erupted in the spring of 1980, large pieces of the mountain (*tear*) _____ away.

8. As a result of the eruption, Mt. St. Helens (*reduce*) _____ from the fifth-tallest mountain in the state of Washington to the thirtieth-tallest.

▼ The actual eruption of a volcano is caused by gas spewing volcanic matter out of the top of the volcano.

Exercise B: Identifying Parenthetically

You often need to give extra information to help your reader stay on track. Often this extra information identifies *who* or *what* you are talking about. Since you don't want the minor information to become the focus of its own sentence, you can often reduce it and add it to a major sentence. We say that this extra information is *parenthetical*.

In the exercise below, add the second sentence of each pair to the first sentence. Reduce it as much as possible and set it off with commas if it is in the middle of the sentence. If it goes at the end, a comma precedes it and a period comes after it.

> EXAMPLE: *Mt. Vesuvius erupted straight up through a central vent.*
> *(Mt. Vesuvius was the volcano that destroyed Pompeii in A.D. 79.)*
>
> Mt. Vesuvius, the volcano that destroyed Pompeii
> in A.D. 79, erupted straight up through a central
> vent.

1. *Reforestation* is the only way to maintain the world's supply of wood. (*Reforestation* is the process of planting new trees to replace older ones that have been cut down or destroyed.)

   _____

   _____

2. The eruption of *Mount Pinatubo* is an example of nature's awesome power. (*Mount Pinatubo* is a volcano in the Philippines that erupted in June of 1991.)

   _____

   _____

3. The explanation for *sudden infant death syndrome* (SIDS) seems to lie in the developing brain. (*SIDS* is a mysterious malady that kills 8,000 babies in the U.S. each year.)

   _____

   _____

4. One of the immediate causes of heart disease is *arteriosclerosis*. (*Arteriosclerosis* is the process by which the arteries harden.)

_____

_____

5. Much of the human body's genetic information is stored in *DNA*. (*DNA* is the master chemical of heredity.)

_____

_____

6. Caterpillars become butterflies through *metamorphosis*. (*Metamorphosis* is a process of physical transformation.)

_____

_____

7. *Pavlov* studied stimulus-response behavior. (*Pavlov* was a Russian physiologist.)

_____

_____

8. *Dynamite* was invented in 1867 by Alfred Nobel. (*Dynamite* is a powerful explosive.)

_____

_____

Exercise C: Writing Chronologically

Use the following words to write seven or eight sentences about the *life cycle of a plant*:

first	*subsequently*
then	*later*
at this point	*finally*
afterwards	

Try to include all of the information from the chart on the facing page (127). Combine some of the stages if you wish. Write in paragraph form. All of your sentences together will describe the life cycle of a plant.

_____

_____

_____

_____

_____

_____

_____

_____

_____

_____

_____

_____

_____

_____

The life cycle of a plant:

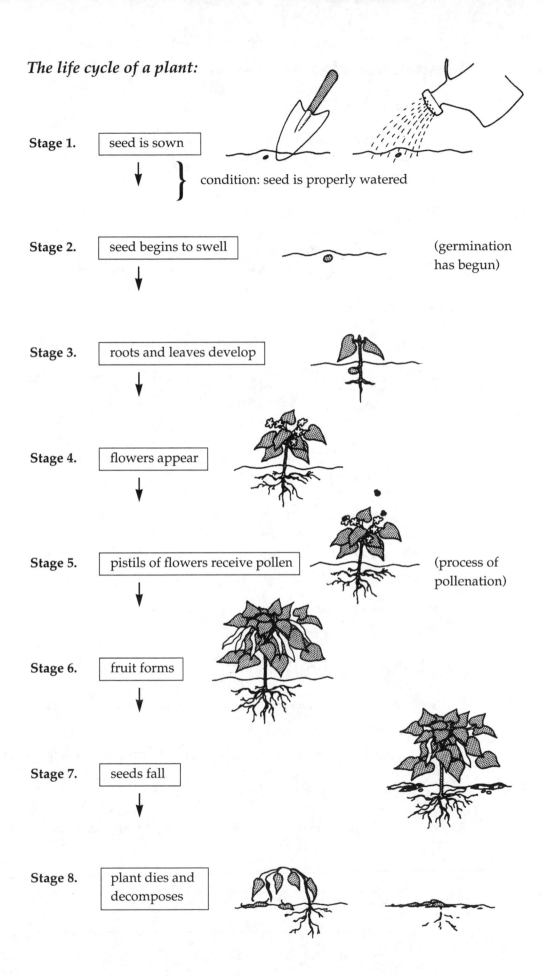

Stage 1. | seed is sown

condition: seed is properly watered

Stage 2. | seed begins to swell

(germination has begun)

Stage 3. | roots and leaves develop

Stage 4. | flowers appear

Stage 5. | pistils of flowers receive pollen

(process of pollenation)

Stage 6. | fruit forms

Stage 7. | seeds fall

Stage 8. | plant dies and decomposes

Exercise D: Citing Examples

Part I

General processes are often more interesting to read about if a writer includes specific examples. In that way, a reader gets more involved. Different ways to include examples are as follows:

A. _____X_____ . *Y is an example (of X).*

> EXAMPLE: *Most volcanos erupt straight up through a central vent. Mt. Vesuvius erupted in this manner. (Mt. Vesuvius* is an example.)

B. *. . . X, such as Y, . . .*

> EXAMPLE: *Some volcanos, such as Mt. Vesuvius, erupt without warning.*

C. _____X_____ . *For example/instance, Y . . .*
_____X_____ . *Y, for example/instance, . . .*

> EXAMPLE: *The eruption of a volcano is one of the earth's most spectacular displays of energy. Mt. St. Helens, for example, released more energy than the atomic bomb that destroyed Hiroshima, Japan.*

In the exercise below, use patterns A, B, or C to add examples. The information in parentheses gives you the example. In some, you may need a whole sentence; in others, you may only need a phrase. The grammar of the sentences already there will help you decide.

Note: The word *like* does not introduce an example. It means *similar to, resembling, having the characteristics of.*

> EXAMPLE: *He works like a horse.*

---

1. Normal cells are *law-abiding*. They reproduce only as often as necessary and then stop. In contrast, abnormal cells, _____ , are *lawbreakers*. They grow and divide without limit. (*cancer cells*)

2. Windstorms occur when masses of hot and cold air come into contact. (*a tornado*)

_____

_____

3. In the process of evolution, a single ancestor can give rise to a number of different species. (*horse, donkey, and zebra—different species with a common ancestor*)

_____

_____

4. Plant nutrition starts when carbon dioxide, water, and various inorganic substances are taken in. From these materials, the plant manufactures the substances it needs. (*sugars, starches, and proteins—substances manufactured by plants*)

_____

_____

5. Some volcanos, _____ , erupt laterally. (*Mt. St. Helens*)

Part II

Add your own examples to the following sentences. Place your examples in separate sentences.

══

1. The element *mercury* is useful in modern science._____ _____

_____

2. Learning to balance is fundamental to mastering other physical skills.

_____

_____

3. Metamorphosis is a process of physical transformation. _____

_____

Exercise E: Stating the Controlling Idea

One of the most important transitions in a composition is the movement from the general topic to a controlling idea. Generally, the introduction narrows to a controlling idea, which then flows into the body.

Introduction:

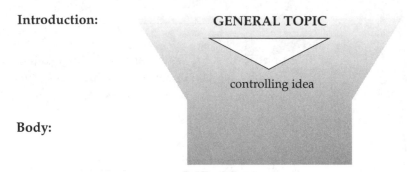

GENERAL TOPIC

controlling idea

Body:

In the exercise below, complete the introduction to each essay by writing one or two sentences stating a controlling idea. Part of the body is included to let you know how the composition would continue.

EXAMPLE ESSAY: **The Eruption of Volcanos**

The eruption of a volcano is one the earth's most spectacular displays of energy. It often releases enough energy to send millions of tons of volcanic dust into the atmosphere.
<u>The power released at the top of a volcano is generated far below the earth's surface.</u>

Fifty to a hundred miles beneath the surface, hot molten rock mixes with gas to create magma, which collects in a chamber. Gradually, . . .

Note: The writer begins with the general powerfulness of a volcano, then moves to the action of releasing that power, and finally gets to the real point—the process of generating that power. As a reader, you perceive the controlling point after you see the direction in which the writer is developing the body.

Essay 1. *Arteriosclerosis*

Heart disease is the number one cause of death in the United States. In order to understand heart disease, it is necessary to know something about coronary artery disease, the immediate cause of heart disease. If the coronary arteries, the vessels on the surface of the heart that carry blood to the heart, do not allow enough blood to pass through, then the heart is in trouble. The first sign of coronary artery disease is a slow process called arteriosclerosis, or hardening of the arteries.

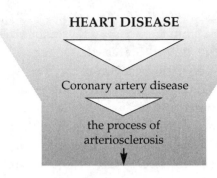

HEART DISEASE

Coronary artery disease

the process of arteriosclerosis

_____

_____

First, the lining of an artery suffers a small injury from the movement of the heart muscle itself, from some strong substance in the blood, or from high blood pressure. Next . . .

Essay 2. *A Water Tap*

A water tap is a simple device for regulating the flow of water. Yet, without water taps, we would have no access to water in our kitchens or bathrooms. The most important parts of a tap are a rod with a handle at the top and a washer fixed to the bottom of the rod.

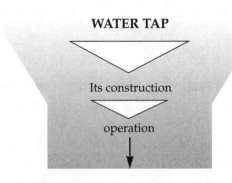

WATER TAP

Its construction

operation

_____

_____

_____

As the handle is turned, the rod rises or descends on spiral threads. If the handle is turned so that the column descends as far as it can go, the washer fits firmly on its seat to close the tap. No water can then flow out. If the handle is turned . . .

Essay 3. *Legionnaires' Disease*

In the summer of 1976, a mysterious disease broke out in the United States. It was a pneumonia-like infection of the lungs. Before the disease was under control, 29 people had died and another 181 had become seriously ill. The only thing these people had in common was their association with the Bellevue-Stratford Hotel in Philadelphia. Most of the 210 had stayed at the hotel while attending an American Legion Convention there; a few had only walked by the entrance. Even after investigators finally discovered the infectious bacteria that had caused the disease, they were baffled by one important question.

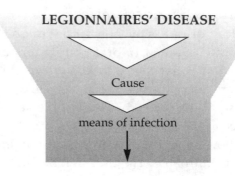

LEGIONNAIRES' DISEASE

Cause

means of infection

_____

_____

First, the bacteria grow in a damp place, such as the cooling tower of a large air-conditioning system. The Bellevue-Stratford had such a cooling tower. From there, they can be carried . . .

Preliminary Writing

You and your teacher can decide which of the following activities to do. Write in your journal or in a special notebook.

1. Make a list of some of the most awesome processes in nature. Choose one and make some notes about the steps or stages in the process.

2. Think back to your childhood and try to remember a process or procedure (natural, mechanical, social, etc.) that mystified you until you figured it out. Write about the process or procedure. What was it? How did you figure it out? What did you figure out?

3. Write briefly about a process that you now understand differently from the way you understood it as a child. How did you understand it then? When did your understanding begin to change? How do you understand it now?

4. Invent a machine to do something that you hate doing. Describe the machine and describe how it works. Use your imagination.

5. Briefly write a description of how a FAX machine works. Let your description "send" a letter from one location to another.

Instructions for Composition 7

Follow the instructions below as you prepare to write your own composition.

1. Choose a process or procedure that you are familiar with or that you can find information on. Describe how it works. It might be a mechanical process, such as the operation of a bicycle pump. (Describe what happens, not how to use it.) It might be a natural process, such as the growth of a seed. It might be a scientific procedure, such as electrolysis. It might be a social or legal process, such as divorce. Check the suggested topics on the following page for ideas.

   Some topics will require you to use passive constructions; others will not. For example, a volcano "erupts;" it is not "erupted." Some topics will involve people; some will not. Remember that you are not instructing anyone to do anything; you are describing how something is done, how it works by itself, or how it happens.

2. In note form, separate your process into steps or stages. Describe which steps are in sequence and which ones are simultaneous. Choose supporting details to go with each one. Define your terms. (Assume that the reader knows nothing about the process.)

3. Write a draft of your composition. Then read through it several times, making changes as you go. More ideas will come to mind as you work. Ask a classmate to read a draft and tell you if something seems unclear.

4. Prepare a clean draft after your changes. Double-check margins and paragraph indentation. Be sure you have a title. Double-check spelling, punctuation, and capital letters. Let your teacher know when your clean draft is ready.

Suggested Topics for Composition 7

Your teacher will ask you to write one or more process descriptions to explain how something works. Here are some suggested topics:

Composition A

Describe a process that is part of your everyday life. If it requires some technical knowledge, do some research. The process itself will be the focus of your composition, but place the process in a setting: home, office, school, etc. If there is reason for humor, be humorous. Here are some ideas:

1. Describe the registration procedure at your school. (You can describe it as it *was* at the beginning of this semester, or as it always *is*.)

2. Describe how a cigarette lighter works.

3. Describe how a toilet flushes.

4. Describe the procedure that you and your family have worked out for sharing something, such as the family car. How does your system work?

5. If you have bought something on credit, describe the credit system that you agreed to. How does it work?

6. Describe how a bicycle pump works.

7. If you have ever applied for and received a loan, scholarship, or grant, describe the procedure that you followed.

Composition B

Describe a process that requires your special cultural perspective.

1. Describe the system of courtship in your culture. How does it work? Who can see whom? Who makes the introductions? When? Under whose supervision? For how long?

2. Describe a mechanical procedure that seems (or seemed) especially difficult, unusual, stupid, wonderful, or technologically impressive. Choose the operation of a machine, a device, or an instrument that is (or was) *new* to you (an electric can opener, a coin changer, a check-cashing machine, etc.). How does it work? What is so unusual about its operation?

3. Describe a procedure that used to seem very commonplace to you, but now seems unusual. Perhaps it is a part of your native culture and now seems unusual because you are in a different culture and you see your native culture with *new eyes*.

Composition C

Describe a process or procedure about which you have special knowledge. Do some research if necessary.

1. Describe how a tadpole changes into a frog, or how a caterpillar changes into a butterfly (*metamorphosis*). (See photo below—check any basic biology or zoology textbook for details.)

2. Describe how plants use sunshine to synthesize organic materials (*photosynthesis*). (Check any basic biology or botany textbook for details.)

3. Describe how babies learn to talk (*language acquisition*). Perhaps you have experience being around young children, such as nieces and nephews or your own children or siblings. Draw on your experience. (You might also look under "early childhood development" or "first language acquisition" in your school library.)

▲ Describe how a caterpillar changes into a butterfly.

UNIT 8

Observing *Cause* and *Effect*

Mt. St. Helens after the eruption ▶

Composition Focus:	*Cause and effect*
Organizational Focus:	*Partition*
Grammatical Focus:	*Parallel constructions*

Study the photo and maps below.

● How does Map A relate to Map B?
● Where and what is Mt. St. Helens?
● What happened there? How serious was it?

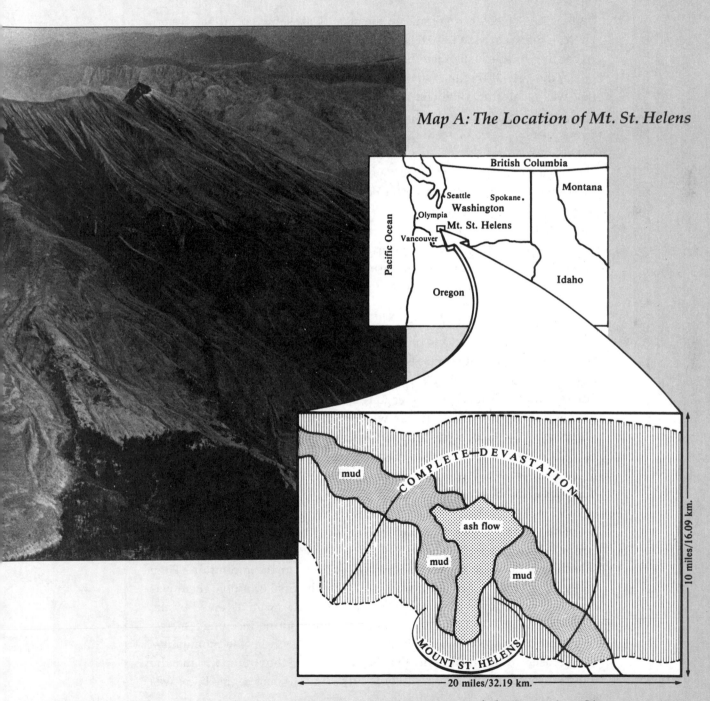

Map A: The Location of Mt. St. Helens

Map B: An Enlargement of the Eruption Site

THE DAY A MOUNTAIN DIED

(1)   Mt. St. Helens is a volcano in the state of Washington in the western United States. On May 18, 1980, it erupted with the force of a nuclear bomb. According to scientists, there had been no volcanic eruption to equal this one in the last 4,000 years. When Mt. St. Helens exploded, it released energy that was greater than the bomb that destroyed Hiroshima, Japan, in 1945. The force was strong enough to send 100 million tons of dust into the atmosphere. A force that strong had tremendous effects on the area around the volcano.

(2)   The visible effects were awesome. Once there had been green meadows and thick forests; after the eruption, there was black volcanic rock and ash. From the air, thousands of acres of trees looked like scattered matchsticks. (See the photo that follows.) Where there had once been clear streams and lakes, there were only bubbling pools of mud. Over 200 kilometers of streams and 26 lakes were destroyed. Once the mountain had stood tall; afterwards, most of its top and all of its north side were missing. The force of the eruption reduced the mountain from the fifth-tallest in the state to the thirtieth-tallest.

(3)   The economic effects on the area were staggering. The U.S. Forest Service estimated that hundreds of millions of dollars' worth of timber was destroyed, more than enough wood to build 200,000 houses. Businesses and homes simply disappeared under tons of rock, ash, and mud. Nearly 300 homes along the Toutle River were badly damaged or destroyed. The port of Portland, sixty miles to the south, was clogged with mud and ash. Because the port was clogged, cargo ships could neither load nor unload and sat helpless. Economists estimated the commercial and personal damages in the billions of dollars.

(4)   Finally, the effects on human life were tragic. Thirty-four bodies were recovered in the weeks following the eruption; twenty-seven more people simply disappeared. Some of the sixty-one were photographers and scientists who were there to record the stirring of the mountain. They thought that there would be a warning before the final eruption; there was none. Other victims were campers and workers who were deceived by the apparent calm of the mountain that bright, sunny spring morning. One—a crusty, old man who owned a little resort five miles from the mountain— had refused to leave. He said that he was part of the mountain and the mountain was part of him. His words turned out to be true; his body was never found.

(5)   All in all, it is impossible to calculate the total effects of the eruption. It will take thousands of years for the geographical damage to be erased. The economy of the area will perhaps never recover. Businesses have closed, never to reopen; the lakes and rivers, which had attracted visitors, are gone forever; the logging industry has no trees to cut. Human life, of course, can never be replaced.

Trees were scattered like matchsticks by the blast.

Complete the outline below with information from Reading 8. Add letters to the outline as you need them.

Effects of the Eruption of Mt. St. Helens

   I. Physical damage

   II. Economic damage

   III. Loss of life

Notes and Questions on Reading 8

Let your teacher guide you through the following notes and questions.

1. A single cause can produce a single effect. For example, *you are hungry* (effect) *because your forgot to eat lunch* (cause). A single cause can also produce multiple effects. For example, *you cut your arm and bruised your leg* (effects) *when you fell down* (cause). (In addition, there can be multiple causes and a single effect.)

2. Writers have different ways of relating cause and effect:

   a) Writers can use special sentence patterns and cause-effect vocabulary, as you will see in Exercise A. For example, *the accident was due to the driver's failure to stop at a red light* (effect + *be due to* + cause).

   b) Writers can also show cause and effect simply by putting sentences next to each other. For example: *My friend received wonderful news from home; he cried when he read the letter.* In other words, reading the good news caused him to cry. Writers sometimes use this technique to create humor. For example: *I quit my job with the ABC Co. two years ago; last year, the company went bankrupt!*

   c) Writers can show cause and effect through simple explanation. For example: *Drugs have devastating effects on the life of an addict. They can bankrupt him, destroy his marriage, and ruin his health.*

   Look at Reading 8. How does the writer relate the cause to the effects (a, b, or c above)?

3. There are many different ways to organize cause and effect. Reading 8 illustrates a very common way. The following questions will help you discern the plan.

   What does the introduction cover (cause or effects)? Does the controlling idea focus on the cause or the effects? Does the body discuss the cause or effects? The conclusion is a summary: Is it a summary of cause or effects? Now you understand one way of developing a cause-effect essay: multiple effects and one cause, with the focus on the effects.

4. There is one last point to bring to your attention: the use of parallel sentences in the body of Reading 8. There, parallel sentences are used to emphasize the contrast between the time before and after the eruption. Pick out as many parallel sentences as you can find.

Before going on to the exercises, tell your classmates if you or your family have ever experienced a natural disaster such as a volcanic eruption. Have you heard stories from your parents or grandparents about floods, tornados, cyclones, fires, etc.?

Exercise A: Stating Cause and Effect

Writers can state cause and effect in different ways:

A. Cigarette smoking ⌈causes⌉ lung cancer.

B. Lung cancer ⌈is caused by⌉ cigarette smoking.

C. ⌈One of the immediate causes of⌉ lung cancer ⌈is⌉ cigarette smoking.

D. Lung cancer ⌈is due to⌉ cigarette smoking.

E. ⌈If⌉ people smoke heavily, they may develop lung cancer.

F. My neighbor, Mr. Peterson, has smoked for many years. ⌈As a consequence,⌉ he may develop lung cancer.

G. ⌈Because⌉ Maria Lopez smoked for many years, she now has lung cancer.

Use the constructions above (A–G) to write cause and effect sentences below. Write two sentences for each. Try to use all of the patterns at least twice.

1. poor diet . . . . health problems

_____

_____

_____

_____

2. drinking . . . . automobile accidents

_____

_____

_____

_____

3. factory smoke and automobile exhaust . . . . air pollution

_____

_____

_____

_____

4. arteriosclerosis and cholesterol buildup . . . . heart disease

_____

_____

_____

_____

5. drinking . . . . liver disease

_____

_____

_____

_____

6. dry scalp . . . . dandruff

_____

_____

_____

_____

7. war . . . . death and human suffering

_____

_____

_____

_____

8. divorce and family breakups . . . . emotional damage to children

_____

_____

_____

_____

9. surplus of consumer goods . . . . lower prices

_____

_____

_____

_____

10. overeating . . . . obesity

_____

_____

_____

_____

Exercise B: Punctuating with Semicolons

In order to show a close relationship, parallel sentences are often combined by means of a semicolon. Clauses with semicolons between them are always _coordinating clauses_; one is not more general or more specific than the other.

> EXAMPLES: _Applicants for jobs must look neat and clean; they must also be prompt._ (similar aspects)
> _Before the eruption, the mountain had stood tall; afterwards, most of its top was missing_ (contrasting aspects)

Read through the sentences below and change periods (.) to semicolons (;) wherever possible. The periods are correct, but semicolons will emphasize a close coordinating relationship.

Note: If the relationship between the sentences does not make a semicolon possible, leave the punctuation as it is. If you use a semicolon, the first letter of the following word is _not_ capitalized.

1. Under the former government, the boulevards were smooth and lined with flowering trees. Under the new regime, they are potholed and lined with trash.

2. Before her tragic accident, the famous skier was full of laughter. Now, she is silent.

3. The effects of the eruption were awesome. Green meadows and thick forests were replaced by tons of volcanic rock and ash.

4. Before the war, the countryside was scattered with neat, wooden farmhouses and cultivated fields. Afterwards, only the blackened foundations of the houses and fields full of weeds remained.

5. Pneumonia is the fifth leading cause of death in the United States. It most often strikes people whose bodies have been weakened by other physical problems.

6. When I was younger, I thought that my parents had all the answers. I thought they were always right.

7. In some countries, education is a privilege. In others, it is considered a right.

8. Mt. St. Helens is a volcano that erupted in Washington state in May 1980. According to scientists, there had not been such a powerful volcanic eruption in 4,000 years.

9. A volcanic eruption can change the geography of an area. Trees, rivers, lakes, fields, and harbors can be destroyed.

10. War can totally devastate a country. The economic base can be destroyed and people's lives shattered.

▲ Describe the effects of World War II on St. Lô, a small town in France, as depicted in this photo.

Exercise C: Partitioning Effects

In the exercise below, think of at least three different types of effects for each of the causes. Phrase the types of effects in parallel constructions.

> EXAMPLE: *the effects of war (on a country):*
> a. effects on human life
> b. effects on the economy
> c. effects on the physical appearance of the countryside

1. the effects of *water pollution* (on whomever or whatever depends on the water):
   a. _____
   b. _____
   c. _____

2. the effects of *winning a million-dollar lottery* (on the winner):
   a. _____
   b. _____
   c. _____

3. the effects of *poor prenatal care* (on a baby):
   a. _____
   b. _____
   c. _____

4. the effects of *divorce* (on a family):
   a. _____
   b. _____
   c. _____

5. the effects of *immigrating to a new country* (on the immigrant):
   a. _____
   b. _____
   c. _____

Exercise D: Making Transitions Within the Body

To subdivide the body of a cause-effect essay into *types* of effects, a writer needs to write a transition sentence (or two) to begin each subdivision. Study the examples below to see how these transition sentences might look.

> EXAMPLE: *The body of an essay on a* **volcanic eruption** *might be subdivided as follows:* **effects on the landscape**, **effects on the economy**, *and* **effects on human life**. *Write one sentence to introduce each type of effect. (In parentheses, note the kind of details to follow each transition.)*
>
> a. First, the massive eruption devastated the surrounding countryside for 200 square miles.
>   *(Followed by details of effects on the landscape—on rivers, lakes, etc.)*
>
> b. Next, the already-fragile economy suffered a staggering blow. *(Followed by economic details—jobs lost, businesses closed, etc.)*
>
> c. Finally, the eruption cost dozens of people their lives. *(Followed by details of effects on human life—number of deaths, individuals who died, etc.)*

Note: Use transition words such as *first, further,* and *finally* to help the reader follow your meaning. Parallel constructions and repeated words can also link your meaning.

---

1. The body of a cause-effect composition on a *country at war* might be subdivided into the following: *effects on the economy, effects on human life, effects on the landscape,* and *effects on politics*. Write one sentence to *move* the composition into each type of effect. (**Note:** You choose the time—the war is raging now or it ended some time ago.)

   a. _____

   _____

   _____

   b. _____

   _____

   _____

   c. _____

   _____

   _____

d. _____

_____

_____

2. The body of a cause-effect composition on *drug addiction and its effects on the addict* might be subdivided into the following: *physical effects*, *psychological effects*, and *social/economic effects*. Write one sentence to *move* the composition into each type of effect. (**Note:** You might be writing about any drug addict or a specific person who is or was addicted.)

a. _____

_____

_____

b. _____

_____

_____

c. _____

_____

_____

Exercise E: Introducing Your Composition

There are different ways to introduce a composition, but any introduction must accomplish the same goal: It must "open the door" for the reader. It must also move the reader into the body—the main part. As a writer, you must know the shape of the body before you can mold the introduction to fit. (That's why writers often write their introductions *after* they write everything else.)

Many formal compositions begin with objective, straightforward statements of the general topic and then narrow to the controlling idea. This is the kind of introduction you find in Reading 8: *the eruption of Mt. St. Helens > the force produced tremendous effects.*

Although Reading 8 is only moderately scientific, it would be possible for a writer to focus more on the human aspects of the event by beginning with a narrative introduction. See how the following introduction drastically changes the tone.

Revised Introduction to Reading 8:

> On the morning of May 18, 1980, David Johnston, a thirty-year-old, blond-bearded geologist for the United States Geological Survey, shouted into his shortwave radio, "Vancouver! Vancouver! This is it!" These words announced the eruption of Mt. St. Helens. They were his last. The explosion blew his trailer off the mountain and into a neighboring valley. His body was never found.
>
> Twenty-six other bodies were never found, either. All in all, sixty-one people died—mostly campers, photographers, scientists, and loggers. This tragic loss of life was only one of the many effects of the powerful eruption . . . .

In the exercise below, practice writing two different introductions to each type of composition outlined for you. Your introductions can be true in fact, or you can make up information. Use your own paper.

1. You are writing a cause-effect composition on *immigration to a new country* and its *effects on the immigrants*. Immigration can cause numerous types of effects: *language problems, economic hardship*, and *mental stress*. The body of your composition is subdivided into the types of effects; whichever comes first will influence the direction of your introduction. Write two different introductions. One might be personal—about you or someone you know; the other might be more formal and objective.

2. You are writing a cause-effect composition on *divorce* and its *effects on a family*. Divorce can create certain effects: *mental stress, economic hardship, stress on the parent-child relationship, inability of the husband and wife to communicate*, and *possible changes in the social standing of the family*. Write two separate introductions. Experiment with your effect on the reader. In one, you might be the child of divorced parents and you personally know the anguish of divorce. In the other, you might be writing to inform fellow divorce counselors.

Preliminary Writing

You and your teacher can decide which of the following activities to do. Write in your journal or in a special notebook.

1. Make a list of the possible causes that could make you quit school, quit your job, and leave town. Use your imagination.

2. You have just won a million-dollar lottery. Congratulations! Write briefly about all of the effects this good fortune will/may have on your life. How will your life change? How will you change? What will you do with the money?

3. Think back to a drastic change in your life—either recent or a long time ago. Briefly analyze the cause(s) for this change. Describe the change.

4. You were mountain climbing in the Cascades the morning that Mt. St. Helens erupted. You were far enough away from the eruption to escape with your life, but close enough to see the top of the mountain explode. Briefly describe what happened. Use your imagination. Describe the effects of the eruption. What did you hear? What did you see? How did you feel? What did you think was going on?

5. You are a television reporter at the scene of a disaster—an airplane crash, an earthquake, a fire, etc. You are live—on the air. Write out your report as you would say it to the television audience. Describe the effects that you see and hear all around you. Analyze the cause of this disaster. (After you write out your report, ask your teacher if you can present it to your classmates.)

Instructions for Composition 8

Follow the instructions below as you prepare to write your own composition.

1. Choose a topic that you can examine for its cause(s) and effect(s). It might be easier to choose one with a single cause and multiple effects (as in Reading 8). It can be a topic that is part of your life. For example, *you have taken a certain job and you examine the effects on your life*: *professional effects, economic effects, etc.* It can also be a topic that involves a larger group, or even all of society. For example, *the effects of divorce on a family*. (Check the suggested topics for ideas.)

2. If the effects can be divided into types, then try to develop parallel labels for the effects. Make notes as you think. For example, "economic effects" and "social effects" are linguistically parallel (same grammar, same type of vocabulary), but "social effects" and "how much money a person makes" are not. Plan to develop the body of your composition by dividing it into types of effects.

3. Plan to develop an introduction with the cause. Let the cause build up to the effects. In other words, use the cause to stimulate the reader's interest. Develop the conclusion as a summary of the effects—as in Reading 8—or plan another type of conclusion. You might also develop a conclusion by asking a question, making a dramatic point, giving a quotation, telling an anecdote, or extending your ideas to another subject area. Ask your teacher for examples.

4. Write a draft of your essay. Read through it several times, making changes as you read. New ideas will come to mind as you go, and you may change your mind about points you've already included. Nothing is set in stone at this point. Ask a classmate to read your draft and tell you if everything is clear.

5. When you have made all the necessary changes, prepare a clean draft. Check it over for any last details: Check punctuation, spelling, indentation, capital letters. Be sure that you have a title. Let your teacher know when your clean draft is ready.

▲ Describe some of the effects of pollution on wildlife.

Suggested Topics for Composition 8

Your teacher will ask you to write one or more cause-effect compositions. Here are some suggested topics:

Composition A

Examine the effects of some action that you once took. Perhaps the action affected only you; maybe it also affected your family, friends, and associates. Describe the action. Tell the reader what kinds of effects this action produced. Tell whom the action affected. Give examples and details. Here are some ideas:

1. Examine the effects of moving away from your family and living without them.

2. Examine the effects of leaving your home country (with or without your family) and living in a new culture.

3. Examine the effects (on you and your situation) of learning a new language.

4. Examine the effects on your life of changing jobs, or taking a certain kind of job.

5. Examine the effects on your life of a particular decision that you once made. (Maybe the effects were all in the past, or perhaps there are still present effects from a past decision.)

Composition B

Examine the effects of some event or action on groups of people. Draw on your experience and your knowledge. If possible, also talk to others in order to profit from their experience and knowledge—and to help you formulate your own ideas. Do some research if necessary. Give examples and details. Here are some ideas:

1. Examine the effects of divorce on a family. Overall, what are the different types of effects? What are the effects on the children? What are the effects on the wife and husband? etc.

2. Examine the effects of war or revolution on a country. What are the types of effects? etc. Give examples of each type.

3. Examine the effects of a certain type of parents on their children. Describe the type of parents. Describe the kinds of effects. Give examples. You may need to distinguish *inevitable* effects from *probable* effects or *possible* effects.

Composition C

Examine the effects of some cause about which you have special knowledge. Do research to get the facts you need.

1. Examine the broad social effects of drug addiction on individuals and on society. What are the physical effects, the psychological effects, the economic effects, etc.? Be specific; give facts and figures. (Check the *Readers' Guide to Periodical Literature* for recent publications.)

2. Examine the political effects of a change in government somewhere in the world. Choose a country, perhaps your homeland. Research the effects. Be specific; give facts and figures. Analyze the types of effects. (Check recent history books or the *Readers' Guide to Periodical Literature* in your library for recent publications.)

Unit 9

Defining Concepts

Tony DeBlois

Composition Focus: *Definition*

Organizational Focus: *Illustration*

Grammatical Focus: *Complex sentences*

Look at the illustrations and try to figure out the sequence of information.

- What is the overall topic?
- Who is Tony?
- What is his role in the sequence?

Now go back to the individual illustrations and describe what you see in each one.

- What is the role of the musical instruments?
- Does there appear to be a contradiction between Tony's handicaps and his musical talent?

After answering these questions and discussing the overall context, read the text that follows.

A Living Contradiction

(1) **S**eventeen years ago, Tony DeBlois was born blind, mentally retarded, and autistic. He did not seem to have much of a chance. Then, when he was two years old, he began to play tunes on his tiny toy xylophone, perfectly imitating some of the children's tunes he had heard on audiocassette.

(2) Today, Tony plays the piano as well, as a professional pianist. He plays jazz, blues, Broadway songs, ragtime tunes, and classical pieces. After hearing a tune, he can imitate it almost perfectly the first time he plays it. More than that, he can improvise: He can change a classical piece to jazz, a jazz piece to a polka, a polka to a waltz. In addition to the piano, Tony plays the organ, guitar, violin, banjo, recorder, and harmonica. His list of musical idols includes Louis Armstrong, Duke Ellington, Scott Joplin, Bach, Mozart, and Beethoven. How can this be? How can such a severely retarded person be so musically talented?

(3) Tony DeBlois has what is called "savant syndrome." This is a condition in which a mentally retarded person has a highly developed talent of a specific kind. The word *savant* comes from the Latin word *sapere*, "to be wise," and the French word *savoir*, "to know." The person who suffers from this condition is called an "idiot savant," a term that literally means "an unknowing person who knows." This clearly seems to be a contradiction, as is the person to whom the term applies. Tony DeBlois is both mentally retarded *and* a musical genius. In the 1988 movie "Rain Man," Dustin Hoffman plays the role of a mathematical genius who is also mentally retarded and autistic.

(4) Savant syndrome is a mystery to researchers in the fields of medicine and psychology. One person who is studying savant syndrome is Dr. Darold Treffert, a psychiatrist in Wisconsin. He has written a book, *Extraordinary People*, about the syndrome. Dr. Treffert says that he has never seen a musical savant as creative as Tony DeBlois. Most musical savants are limited to simply repeating tunes they hear. Dr. Treffert points out that Tony's ability to improvise is a big step above rote memory. Dr. Treffert plans to continue studying Tony to help expand psychiatry's knowledge of the syndrome.

(5)   As for Tony DeBlois's musical career, he is now earning small fees for playing at nursing homes and centers for senior citizens. He is studying jazz piano at the Music School at Rivers in Weston, Massachusetts, near his home. He is also being considered for admission to the Berklee College of Music, a prestigious music school in Boston. Whether Tony is admitted or not, he will continue to be encouraged by his mother and stepfather, his fiercest allies.

Taking Notes

From your understanding of the reading, from your class discussion, from the visuals that precede the reading, and with some help from your dictionary, define the following:

1. What is *savant syndrome*?

2. What is an idiot savant?

3. What is *autism*?

4. What is a genius?

5. What is *musical improvisation*?

6. What is *rote memory*?

Notes and Questions on Reading 9

Let your teacher guide you through the following notes and questions.

1. In Reading 4, the writer defines "laughter" by identifying it in two ways: as a physical and as a psychological expression. Do you remember?

    What is the author of Reading 9 defining? How does the author get you, the reader, to understand what *X* (the subject) is?

2. Compare Readings 4 and 9. In one, illustration plays a major role as a method of development; in the other, it plays a minor role. Identify which is which.

3. Why do you think the author begins with Tony DeBlois's story? What purpose does his story serve? How does it relate to the author's definition of savant syndrome?

4. Where in the reading does the writer prepare you for the "real" subject of the essay? Find the point of transition from Tony's story into the more generalized subject.

5. How is Reading 9 almost the reverse of traditional essay order—general subject narrowing to the controlling idea and then supported with specifics? How much of Reading 9 consists of supporting specifics? Where are they? How much of the essay is spent on the generalized subject? Where is the general subject developed?

6. How does the essay conclude? What is the connection between the conclusion and the introduction?

Before going on to the exercises, tell your classmates if you have ever met anyone like Tony DeBlois. Had you ever heard of savant syndrome? What strikes you as so unusual about it? Have you seen the movie *Rain Man*? If so, describe and discuss the character of Raymond, played by Dustin Hoffman. (See photo on page 167.)

Exercise A: Emphasizing with *Such* and *So*

Use *such* or *so* in each sentence below, depending on the grammar of the sentence. Both words are used to emphasize, but the grammar of each is slightly different:

such (a/an) (+ADJ.) + NOUN

so ADV. ADJ. (a/an + NOUN)

EXAMPLE: *Take Tony DeBlois. It is amazing that* _____such_____ *a severely retarded person can be* _____so_____ *musically talented.*

1. When Tony DeBlois was born, doctors told his mother that he was _____ retarded that they did not think he would ever acquire language.

2. The news about Tony was _____ a heavy weight to bear that Mrs. DeBlois didn't think she could survive.

3. Tony DeBlois is _____ a talented musician that he is being considered for admission to the Berklee College of Music in Boston.

4. Dustin Hoffman played _____ convincing a role in *Rain Man* that some found it hard to believe that he is not really retarded.

5. In *Rain Man*, Dustin Hoffman played the role of an idiot savant who was _____ mathematically talented that he could look at a box of toothpicks spilled on the floor and give an exact count.

6. Dr. Treffert has never known _____ a creative musical savant as Tony DeBlois.

7. Dr. Treffert has never known _____ creative a musical savant as Tony DeBlois.

8. When Tony was small, he had _____ terrible temper tantrums that his mother had to sit him down on the floor and wrap her arms and legs around him.

9. His temper tantrums were _____ terrible that he was a danger to himself and others. Temper tantrums are one symptom of savant syndrome.

10. It is difficult to understand how the human brain can develop to produce individuals who are _____ limited in most functions but _____ talented in art, music, or mathematics.

Exercise B: Providing Cohesion

Complete the sentences below with words that connect the meaning of one part of each sentence to another. Some words signal the type of information that follows; some words rename what has gone before, by paraphrasing or categorizing. Let your sense of meaning direct you. Not everyone in the class needs to come up with the same words, as long as the sentences make sense.

EXAMPLE: *Dr. Darold Treffert is the author of* Extraordinary People, *a* _____book_____ *about savant syndrome.*

1. Tony DeBlois suffers from savant syndrome. _____ is a condition in which a mentally retarded person has a highly developed talent in a specific area, _____ painting, music, or mathematics.

2. The person who suffers from savant syndrome is called an "idiot savant," a/an _____ that literally means "an unknowing person who knows."

3. Savant syndrome is a mystery to professionals, _____ psychiatrists, geneticists, and neurologists.

4. Tony DeBlois suffers from savant syndrome, a/an _____ in which a retarded individual is highly talented in a specific area.

5. Not only can Tony play any tune he has ever heard, he can also transpose songs and change them to other keys, a/an _____ that not many musical savants have.

6. Tony can play the piano, as well as the organ, guitar, violin, and other musical _____ .

7. Tony can play Broadway songs, ragtime tunes, and classical _____ .

8. Tony idolizes Louis Armstrong, Duke Ellington, Bach, Beethoven, and other _____ of music.

9. Tony can play a tune exactly as he has heard it, but he can do more than simply _____ what he has heard; he can improvise, creating new tunes as he plays.

10. Tony continues to be encouraged by his mother and stepfather, who have been his staunchest _____ .

Exercise C: Identifying Parenthetically

Information that is not central to what a writer wants to say can be embedded in another sentence rather than having its own sentence. The information in parentheses below is not central; add it to the main sentence above it.

> EXAMPLES: *The movie* Rain Man *was about a mathematical savant.* (*The movie starred Dustin Hoffman.*)
>
> The movie *Rain Man*, starring Dustin Hoffman, was about a mathematical savant.

1. Savant syndrome is a condition in which a mentally retarded person has a highly developed talent in a specific area. (Examples of these specific areas are painting, music, and mathematics.) (Note: Use *such as*.)

   _____

   _____

   _____

2. Tony DeBlois plays the guitar, piano, banjo, harmonica, and violin. (Tony is a blind and autistic seventeen-year-old.)

   _____

   _____

   _____

3. Tony DeBlois is at the level of a professional pianist, according to Steven Lipman. (Lipman is director of admissions for the Berklee College of Music in Boston.)

   _____

   _____

   _____

4. Tony can just make up songs and he never writes anything down, according to his mother. (Tony's mother's name is Janice DeBlois.)

_____

_____

_____

5. Tony is more creative than other musical savants who are limited to repeating tunes they hear, according to Dr. Darold Treffert. (Dr. Treffert is the author of *Extraordinary People*. *Extraordinary People* is a book about savant syndrome.)

_____

_____

_____

6. Dr. Treffert was a consultant to the 1988 movie *Rain Man* in which Dustin Hoffman played a mathematical savant. (Dr. Treffert is a psychiatrist in Wisconsin.)

_____

_____

_____

7. One of Tony's musical idols is Louis Armstrong. (Louis Armstrong was a famous jazz trumpeter and band leader.)

_____

_____

_____

8. One of Tony's staunchest allies is his stepfather. (Tony's stepfather's name is Thomas DeBlois.)

_____

_____

_____

Exercise D: Combining Sentences

Please combine each set of sentences below by using the word in parentheses. You will end up with only *one* sentence. You may need to delete some words from the sentences in the set in order to combine them.

1. "I like to play the blues, 'the St. Louis Blues'," says Tony. Tony's list of musical idols includes Dizzy Gillespie, Duke Ellington, and Louis Armstrong. (*whose*)

   _____

   _____

2. Tony began to play tunes on his tiny toy xylophone. He was two years old. (*when*)

   _____

   _____

3. Tony plays well. A professional pianist plays no better than Tony. (*as _____ as*)

   _____

   _____

4. Tony hears a tune. He can then imitate it almost perfectly the very first time he plays it. (*after*)

   _____

   _____

5. Dr. Darold Treffert is studying savant syndrome and wrote a book about it. He served as a consultant to the 1988 movie *Rain Man*. (*who*)

   _____

   _____

6. Dr. Treffert says that he had never met a creative musical savant. That was before he met Tony DeBlois. (*until*)

   _____

   _____

7. Tony may or may not be admitted to the Berklee College of Music. He will continue to be encouraged by his parents. (*whether . . . . or not*)

_____

_____

8. Tony will continue to be encouraged by his parents. They have been his staunchest supporters. (*who*)

_____

_____

Exercise E: Interpreting Meaning

Answer each question below in one or two sentences. Answer in your own words, based on your understanding of Reading 9.

1. Why does the author of Reading 9 say that Tony DeBlois "did not have much of a chance"?

_____

_____

_____

2. Why is Tony's ability to improvise more impressive than his ability to imitate?

_____

_____

_____

3. What is contradictory about the term "idiot savant"?

_____

_____

_____

4. Why does Dr. Darold Treffert consider Tony DeBlois so creative?

_____

_____

_____

5. In your opinion, what role does music play in Tony DeBlois's connection to the world around him?

_____

_____

_____

Preliminary Writing

You and your teacher should decide which of the following activities to do. Write in your journal or a special notebook.

1. Borrow or rent *Rain Man* on video cassette. After seeing it, write about Raymond, the mathematical savant played by Dustin Hoffman. What characterizes his behavior? What are his talents; what can he do? What more do you understand about savant syndrome?

2. Make a list of eight or ten physical or mental handicaps. After you've made your list, pick out two or three to define. Write brief definitions.

3. Think of individuals, famous or not, whose stories could illustrate something about the handicaps in 2 above. Write down what they illustrate. Be as precise as you can.

4. Define "creativity." Who do you know who is "creative"? How is this person creative? What are other ways in which creativity can be expressed? Are there different kinds of creativity? Is it learned or innate in your opinion? Write a brief paragraph.

5. Define "intelligence." Write a brief paragraph. What does the term mean to you? When do you consider a person "intelligent"? What do intelligent people do? What behaviors are "unintelligent," in your opinion? What words do you consider to be the opposite of "intelligent"?

Instructions for Composition 9

Please follow the instructions below as you write:

1. Choose a topic that you can define by telling about someone or something. This topic might be a personal quality, a physical handicap, a certain behavior, etc. (Check the topics in the following section for ideas.)

2. After you choose your topic, decide *who* or *what* (a person, an event, an act, etc.) can illustrate your subject. Make notes as you think. Jot down words and ideas that come to mind as you think about your subject to be defined or your illustration.

3. Look back over your notes. Draw circles around whatever you want to build into your composition.

4. Write a draft of your composition. Read through it several times to see what needs to be included, what needs to be left out, and what needs more work. Work it over. Read through it again. If possible, let a classmate read it to see if everything is clear.

5. When you're satisfied with the content of your composition, write a clean draft. Check it for spelling, punctuation, margins, capital letters, and paragraph indentation. Add a title. Tell your teacher when your clean draft is ready.

Suggested Topics for Composition 9

Your teacher will ask you to write one or more compositions using illustration as a means of defining.

Composition A

From personal knowledge of people that you have known and whose stories can expand your reader's understanding, define one of the following:

1. dyslexia

2. deafness

3. blindness

4. genius

5. stubbornness

6. optimism

7. courage

8. persistence

9. deceit

10. a certain type of mental illness

Composition B

Define a quality that is highly valued in your culture. Define it by describing the behavior of someone who has/had this quality or define it (negatively) by telling the story of someone who does/did not have it.

The following may be valued qualities that you would like to define:

1. leadership

2. academic success

3. honesty

4. selflessness

5. wisdom

6. kindness

7. perception

8. clairvoyance

9. speaking ability

10. ?

Composition C

Define something about which you have special knowledge. You are the authority and are explaining this subject to the public. Do your research beforehand to get details. Here are some possibilities:

1. Write to the young people in your community about a quality that you fear will be lost. The young will listen to you; they look up to you and respect you. Your message to them will be distributed at a community meeting.

2. Define one of the following to parents who may need to better understand their children:

    a. self-esteem

    b. creativity

    c. intelligence

    d. guilt

    e. positive reinforcement

    f. discipline

    g. expressions of anger

    h. growing independence

    i. rebelliousness

    j. respect

    Use one child's story to help define and illustrate what you mean.

A. Each of these handguns was involved in a murder. In fact, handguns were involved in half of the 23,000 murders committed with firearms in the U.S. last year. ▼

Arguing a *Point*

Composition Focus: *Argumentation*

Organizational Focus: *Induction*

Grammatical Focus: *Complex sentences*

Study the illustrations below.

- What do you see in A? Can you imagine where this display is? What does the caption tell you?
- What do you see in B? What might the child do? What does the caption tell you?
- What do you see in C? Which weapons are the most dangerous? What is a "homicide"?
- What is the point of all three illustrations? Look at the title of Reading 10. How does the title relate to the illustrations?

B. Every year, hundreds of children die from guns kept by their parents for protection. ▼

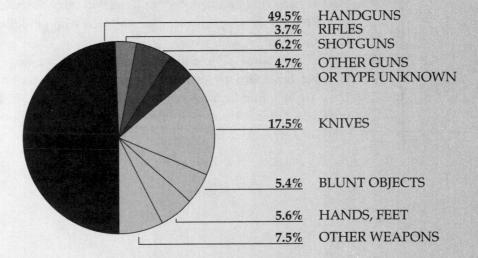

Weapons used in homicides in 1990

49.5%	HANDGUNS
3.7%	RIFLES
6.2%	SHOTGUNS
4.7%	OTHER GUNS OR TYPE UNKNOWN
17.5%	KNIVES
5.4%	BLUNT OBJECTS
5.6%	HANDS, FEET
7.5%	OTHER WEAPONS

C. The death rate is three times higher for robberies at gunpoint than for robberies with knives, the next most dangerous robbery weapon. ▶

BANNING HANDGUNS

(1) A s the United States changed from an undeveloped, underpopulated, and underpoliced frontier civilization into a modern, industrialized country, one vestige remained—the gun. While people discarded their plows, bonnets, and kerosene lamps, they failed to discard their guns.

(2) Guns, especially handguns, are still very much in use today. Since 1963, guns have killed more Americans than were killed in World War II. More than 35 million handguns are in circulation, and Americans keep on buying them at a rate of one every 13 seconds. At the current rate, over 50 million handguns will be in circulation in 50 years.

(3) The United States has the highest rate of murder by guns in the world. In 1990 alone, guns were the cause of death in 64% of the 23,000 murders committed in the U.S. As guns become more available, people are more likely to die during violent crimes.

(4) Many Americans are greatly discouraged by the presence of so many handguns. The United States has no difficulty in regulating CB radios, boat trailers, and dogs, yet it cannot adequately regulate handguns. What is the problem? First, the National Rifle Association is, according to some legislators, the strongest, most effective lobbying organization in Washington, D.C. The NRA opposes government control over handguns, and it is very effective at election time in helping to defeat legislators who favor gun control.

(5) Second, many people see modern society as a continuation of the frontier. There are the "good guys" and the "bad guys," and the good guys must be able to defend themselves against the increasing number of bad guys, the criminals. Guns offer protection; opponents of gun control argue that "if guns are outlawed, only outlaws will carry them." Never mind that it is often the good guys and their children who get killed with the very guns they buy for self-defense.

(6) Third, some people like handguns. They are easy and convenient. Whether handguns are owned for defense or crime, they appeal to people. They are small and can be kept hidden when not in use. They can also be used at a distance from the victim; they keep the user of the gun at a safer range and less involved.

(7)   Many of those arguing against new laws to control handguns say that there are enough laws already. These laws just have to be enforced, they claim. The nation does have laws all right—a jumble of over 25,000 federal, state, and local regulations. These regulations cannot, on the whole, be enforced because they are inconsistent and unclear.

(8)   The nation needs new laws to put handguns out of business. The new laws must, first, be federal laws, not state laws, because handguns are so mobile. Second, the laws must ban handguns altogether, except for use by specially authorized public officials, such as police officers. An individual's presumed right to bear arms must yield to the community's need for safety. Third, the penalty for continuing to possess a handgun after the ban must be severe. The penalty must be especially severe for criminal use of a handgun.

(9)   It is time to get rid of handguns. Now. There is no time to wait. Proposals that fall short of an absolute ban will not work—a waiting period to buy a gun does not keep handguns out of circulation; limits on where and how people can carry guns do not decrease the number; denying access to high-risk people (criminals, minors, etc.) does not keep guns away from those who should not have them. We cannot allow the good guys to own millions of guns and then expect to keep them away from the bad guys. The future of America is at stake. The time of the American frontier is over.

Complete the outline below with information from Reading 10. Add letters as you need them in each division.

Banning Handguns in the U.S.

   I.   Seriousness of the problem

   II. Reasons for the lack of handgun regulation

   III. Solution to the problem

Notes and Questions on Reading 10

Let your teacher guide you through the following notes and questions.

1. You can develop an argument on paper, but you must first develop it in your own head. You, as the person arguing, must have a point of view, a premise to start from. If your basic premise is unsound, your argument will be faulty.

   The following is a clear example of a simple argument based on a false premise:

Major premise:	*All people have green skin.*
Minor premise:	*Alice is a person.*
Conclusion:	*Therefore, she has green skin.*

   The argument in Reading 10 is much more complex, to say the least. The logic goes something like this:

Major premise:	*Any threat to public safety should be removed.*
Minor premise:	*Guns threaten public safety.*
Conclusion:	*Therefore, guns should be removed (banned).*

   Most people agree with the major premise above, which is implied but not directly stated in Reading 10. The public disagreement is over the minor premise. Therefore, not everyone agrees with the conclusion.

2. In argumentation, almost more than in any other type of writing, the writer is strongly involved with the reader (the audience). The writer wants to affect the audience in three possible ways: change their attitude by getting them to understand a problem, change their behavior by getting them to act, or both.

   What about Reading 10? Does the writer try to affect attitude, behavior or both?

3. There are different ways to construct a logical argument. Reading 10 shows one way: The writer deals with the problem and then presents a solution. Let's call Reading 10 a problem-solution argument.

   Look back at Reading 10. When does the writer begin to discuss the problem? Why do you think the writer discusses it with statistics? How does the writer continue the discussion of the problem (fourth paragraph)? How long does the discussion of the problem last?

   Where does the writer begin to discuss the solution? When does the writer get to the crucial point—the conclusion to the argument? This conclusion is really the controlling idea of the composition and gives the text its title.

   Because the controlling idea is at the end and not in its usual position at the beginning of the composition, the argument is said to be "inductive." Turned around, with the conclusion stated as a generalization at the beginning, the argument would be "deductive." Organized either way, good arguments look something like this:

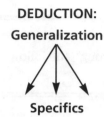

DEDUCTION:

Generalization

Specifics

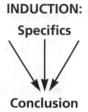

INDUCTION:

Specifics

Conclusion

4. Arguments often end with a call for action, if the writer's aim is to affect behavior. How does Reading 10 end? What is the audience supposed to do?

Before going on to the exercises, discuss your ideas on gun control with your classmates. Are you for it or against it? Do you own a gun? Do you know people who carry guns? Why do they do so? Do people in your homeland carry guns?

Exercise A: Combining Sentences

Each conjunction below establishes a special relationship between the ideas that it connects.

EXAMPLES: *yet*   *The United States became a modern, industrialized country, yet it retained one vestige of the frontier—the gun.* (*Yet*: One clause is in contrast to the other.)

whether . . . (or)   *In the United States, it is now legal to buy a handgun, whether it is to be used for lawful or criminal purposes.* (*Whether . . . (or)*: One clause contains alternative conditions for the other.)

as   *As settlers moved West, they needed guns in order to obtain food and protect themselves.* (*As*: One clause is in the same period of time as the other.)

because   *Many people own guns because they believe that guns offer them protection.* (*Because*: The clause following the conjunction states the reason for the other clause.)

In the exercise below, use one of the four conjunctions above to combine each pair of sentences. Write out the combination.

1. People who are against new laws to control handguns point to the existing laws. These laws cannot be enforced.

   _____

   _____

2. The existing handgun regulations cannot be enforced. They are inconsistent and unclear.

   _____

   _____

3. The United States developed into a modern country. One vestige of the early frontier days remained. (**Note:** *Time* is important here.)

   _____

   _____

4. Handguns are widely owned. They appeal to people.

   _____

   _____

5. The U.S. government has no difficulty in regulating automobiles. It cannot adequately regulate handguns.

   _____

   _____

6. It is legal to buy a handgun. It will be used for self-defense or for a criminal purpose.

   _____

   _____

Exercise B: Writing Sentences of Comparison

Rewrite the first sentence of each pair below as a comparison. The second sentence gives you the necessary information. Use either comparative or superlative grammar.

Superlative grammar

the _____ -est

the most _____

Comparative grammar

_____ -er than

more _____ than

EXAMPLE: *The United States has a high rate of murder by guns. (No other country in the world has a higher rate.)*

The United States has the highest rate of murder by guns in the world.

1. The United States is politically stable, yet internally violent. (Many other countries are less politically stable and less internally violent.)

   _____

   _____

2. The National Rifle Association is a strong, effective lobbying organization. (No other lobbying organization in Washington, D.C., seems stronger or more effective.)

   _____

   _____

3. The United States does a good job of regulating CB radios, boat trailers, and dogs. (The U.S. doesn't do such a good job of regulating handguns.)

   _____

   _____

4. People believe that guns offer protection. (They feel that knives and other weapons offer less protection.)

   _____

   _____

Exercise C: Analyzing Arguments

Read the arguments below and answer the questions about each one. There are two possible aspects to each argument—*problem* and *solution*—but they are not always equally developed. The solution might be carefully explained, but the problem only implied. Alternatively, the problem might be explained, and the solution only implied. Write your answers to the questions below; you do not need to write complete sentences.

Argument A: Illegal Aliens

Congress should pass stricter laws to discourage foreigners from entering the United States to work illegally. These laws could control workers by requiring every person who works legally to carry an identification card. They could control employers by making it illegal for any employer to hire a worker without first checking his or her I.D. card. With these two laws in effect, aliens without I.D. cards would find it impossible to get jobs. They would then be more likely to return to their own countries. It is in the interest of everyone who is working legally to support the passage of these laws. Congress should act now.

1. What is the problem? _____

   Is it implied or directly stated? _____

2. What is the solution to the problem? _____

   Is it implied or directly stated? _____

3. What will the solution accomplish? _____

   _____

4. How will the solution accomplish its goals? _____

   _____

5. What will the effects of the solution be? _____

   _____

Argument B: Cancer Research

Much of the cancer research of the last several decades is in doubt. Cancer researchers have been working with contaminated cell cultures without knowing that the cultures were contaminated. The problem began in the 1950s when researchers got hold of some particularly vigorous cancer cells. Then, through careless laboratory procedures, these vigorous cells began to invade the cells of other cultures used in the same lab. Since cultures are traded from laboratory to laboratory across the country and even around the world, the "outlaw" cells were soon contaminating cell cultures everywhere. Now, researchers may think that they are working with one type of cell when they are actually working with the "outlaw" cancer cells. As a result, many false ideas about cancer have entered medical literature.

1. What is the problem? _____

    Is it implied or directly stated? _____

2. What caused the problem? _____

    _____

3. What solution is very indirectly implied? _____

    _____

Exercise D: Considering the Audience

Reread the arguments in the preceding exercise to figure out the writer's intended effect on the audience. In other words, what do you think the writer wants the reader(s) to do? The following are all possible effects on the audience:

Effect X: The writer wants to change the attitude of the audience. The audience should understand a particular problem.

Effect Y: The writer wants to change the behavior of the audience. That is, the audience should act.

Effect Z: The writer wants to accomplish both X and Y: get the audience to understand and to act.

Answer the questions about Arguments A and B in Exercise C. Refer to X, Y, and Z above to answer some of the questions.

Argument A: Illegal Aliens

1. What is the writer's intended effect: Does the writer want to change the audience's behavior, attitude, or both? What should the audience understand or do?

   _____

   _____

   _____

Argument B: Cancer Research

1. What is the writer's intended effect? Does the writer want to change the audience's attitude, behavior, or both? Write out the intended effect(s).

   _____

   _____

   _____

Exercise E: Reasoning Through an Argument

In any argument, a writer must have specifics to help the audience understand the problem and accept or achieve the solution. These specifics are often in the form of *reasons* why the problem is a problem, why the audience should do something about it, why the solution will solve the problem, etc.

Read the information below and try to come up with three reasons to help achieve each intended effect. You can write out your reasons in complete sentences or list them in note form.

Argument Against Early Marriage

Intended audience: unmarried teenagers

Intended effect: Unmarried teenagers should understand the responsibilities of marriage and should consider waiting until they are older to get married.

Reasoning: What points can you make to help unmarried teenagers understand the responsibilities of early marriage?

1. _____

2. _____

3. _____

Argument Against Cigarette Smoking

Intended audience: cigarette smokers

Intended effect: Cigarette smokers should understand the negative aspects of smoking cigarettes.

Reasoning: What points can you make to help cigarette smokers understand why it is harmful to smoke?

1. _____

2. _____

3. _____

Argument for Banning Handguns

Intended audience:	gun owners who are parents of young children
Intended effect:	They should give up their guns.
Reasoning:	What can you say to make gun owners understand the dangers?

1. _____

2. _____

3. _____

Preliminary Writing

You and your teacher can decide which of the following activities to do. Write in your journal or in a special notebook.

1. You have a friend who chain-smokes. You are worried about your friend's health. Make a list of the reasons you might give to convince him or her to quit smoking.

2. You are concerned about the environment. You think that everyone needs to recycle their plastic, glass bottles and jars, cans, and newspapers. Make a list of the reasons why everyone should recycle.

3. Many people do not recycle because it is not convenient for them. They have to drive to different places to drop off their things. Briefly devise a solution to this problem. Explain it. Tell why it will make recycling easier for people. Your hope is that more people will recycle if they accept your solution.

4. Think back to something that your parents wanted you to do that you did *not* want to do. How did they try to persuade you to do it? Write about it. How could their argument have been more persuasive? Did you do whatever they wanted you to do?

5. Think of something about your class, your classmates, or your teacher that you want to change. What is it? How can you persuade them to change? What do you want to do? How do you want things to be? Write about it. If appropriate, read what you've written to your classmates and teacher. See if they are persuaded by your argument.

Instructions for Composition 10

Follow the instructions below as you prepare to write your own composition.

1. Choose an issue that you can argue. (Check the topics in the following section for ideas.) For the purposes of this lesson, see the issue as a problem. In order to have a full argument, you need three elements: a major premise, a minor premise, and a conclusion. In putting together an argument in your own head, you might start with any one of the three in order to "find" the other two. For example, your thinking might go something like this:

    a.   Senator X, the so-and-so, should be kicked out of office!
    b.   Why? . . . Because he is dishonest!
    c.   So what? . . . Well, no dishonest politician should remain in office.

   Now, you have a full argument! You can formalize it to look like this:

   Major premise: *No dishonest politician should remain in office.*
   Minor premise: *Senator X is dishonest.*
   Conclusion: *Senator X should be removed from office.*

2. Construct your argument as a problem and a solution. Develop your minor premise as a problem (throughout the body). For example, *the dishonest Senator X is the problem.* As you develop the problem, you will have to prove your premise with all the evidence that you can find. For example, cite Senator X's arrest for income tax evasion.

   Develop your logical conclusion as the solution to the problem: *Senator X should be removed from office.* Tell how, when, etc. Tell what benefits will come from the solution. For example, you might claim that public confidence in government will increase.

   Conclude your composition with a call to action. What do you want your audience to do? For example, you might want citizens to send letters to the leader of the Senate asking for Senator X's removal.

   The introduction to your composition, which will probably be composed last, can present your major premise. For example, you might talk about how important it is to have honest public officials.

3. Make notes as you figure out your premises and your solutions. Making notes will help you think.

4. Write a draft of your essay. You may want to leave space for your introduction and come back to it after you compose your conclusion. After you finish your draft, read through it several times to see what you want to change, add, or subtract. Ask a classmate to read it and give you advice.

5. When you have made all the changes that you think improve your essay, prepare a clean draft. Check it over for details before you stop. Let your teacher know when your clean draft is ready.

Suggested Topics for Composition 10

Your teacher will ask you to write one or more essays of argumentation.

Composition A

Argue an issue that is of personal concern to you. Take a problem that is part of your everyday life. Discuss it. What is it? Why is it a problem? How serious a problem is it? Offer a solution. What is the solution? How will it solve the problem? What benefits will come from it? Formulate your ideas in terms of a major premise, minor premise, and conclusion *before* you start writing. Have your classmates or your teacher check your logic. Here are some situations:

1. Your brother is in City X, alone and unhappy. You and the rest of your family are in City Y. You think that your brother should quit his job in City X and move to City Y. You might argue that he will be much happier living with or near his family. In fact, you might think that most people are happier near their families. Direct your argument to a general family audience.

2. Some of the students in your class are not serious about their studies. They disrupt the class by making it necessary for the teacher to repeat the lessons and explanations. The whole class suffers, and you feel angry. Argue that these students should be dropped from the class if they don't work. Direct your argument to a general student audience.

3. You have a problem with the plumbing in your apartment. The faucets drip and the pipe under the bathroom sink leaks. (The landlord pays the water bill, not you.) You think that it is the landlord's responsibility to correct the problem immediately. He doesn't seem to be in a hurry. Argue that it is in *his* interest to fix the plumbing. Direct the argument to your landlord in the form of a letter.

Composition B

Argue an issue that is of concern to a larger group of people—students, residents of a neighborhood, parents of children at a local elementary school, etc. Present a problem, and offer a solution. Give supporting reasons and evidence for your solution. Formulate your argument as a major premise, minor premise, and conclusion *before* you begin writing. Have your classmates or your teacher check your logic.

1. You think that many people get married too young. You want to argue that they should wait until they are older. (If your position is contrary to this one, then argue *your* position.) Direct your argument to young people.

2. It bothers you to see so many old people alone or in special homes for the elderly (often called *nursing homes*). You want to argue that older people should remain with their families, regardless of their physical and mental conditions. (If your point of view is the opposite, then argue that point of view.) Direct your argument to families.

Practice Composition Exam: C

It's time for your last practice test. Pretend that it is a real test, unless your teacher actually decides to make it a real test. You have _____ minutes to write a composition. You may (not) use a dictionary. Follow your teacher's special instructions.

Exam C1: Argue one of the following:
   a. A consumer should always pay cash and not buy on credit.
   b. Elderly parents should (not) live with their grown children and (not) live alone or in nursing homes.
   c. Students should (not) be placed in a language program on the basis of a test score.
   d. Argue a topic chosen by you or your teacher.

Exam C2: Describe how something works (an operational process):
   a   how it rains
   b. how a common machine or mechanical device works (Example: a toaster, a can opener, etc.)
   c. the government procedure for granting visas, political asylum, or green cards
   d. a topic chosen by you or your teacher

Exam C3: Write a cause-effect composition on one of the following:
   a. the effects of living alone
   b. the effects of air or water pollution
   c. the effects of physical exercise
   d. the effects of a topic chosen by you or your teacher

Exam C4: Define one of the following:
   a. a particular human quality
   b. a particular physical handicap
   c. a particular mental handicap
   d. a topic chosen by you or your teacher

PHOTO CREDITS